POPULATION, HEALTH AND DEVELOPMENT IN GHANA:

ATTAINING THE MILLENIUM DEVELOPMENT GOALS

POPULATION, HEALTH AND DEVELOPMENT IN GHANA:

ATTAINING THE MILLENIUM DEVELOPMENT GOALS

Edited by
Chuks J. Mba and Stephen O. Kwankye

SUB-SAHARAN PUBLISHERS

First published in 2007 by
SUB-SAHARAN PUBLISHERS
P.O. BOX LG358,
LEGON, ACCRA, GHANA

© Population Association of Ghana, University of
Ghana, Legon, 2007

ISBN: 978-9988-647-61-2

Typesetting and Graphics by Kwabena Agyepong

CONTENTS

About the Contributors   vii

Acknowledgements   xi

Dedication   xiii

Preface   xv

Chapter 1   1
INTRODUCTION
Stephen O. Kwankye and Chuks J. Mba

Chapter 2   13
**FERTILITY DECLINE IN GHANA:
IMPLICATIONS FOR PUBLIC POLICY**
S. K. Gaisie

Chapter 3   29
**INFANT AND CHILD HEALTH:
EVIDENCE FROM 2003 GHANA
DEMOGRAPHIC AND HEALTH SURVEY**
Emmanuel O. Tawiah

Chapter 4   53
**ADOLESCENT SEXUALITY AND
REPRODUCTIVE HEALTH IN GHANA:
SOME RESULTS FROM A SURVEY
OF CAPE COAST AND MANKRONG**
Stephen O. Kwankye

Chapter 5   91
**POPULATION GROWTH,
WATER/SANITATION AND HEALTH**
S. K. Gaisie and P. G. Gyau-Boakye

v

Chapter 6   135
HIV/AIDS AND SURVIVAL
CHALLENGES IN SUB-SAHARAN AFRICA:
AN ILLUSTRATION WITH GHANA
AND SOUTH AFRICA
Chuks J. Mba

Chapter 7   163
WOMEN'S EMPOWERMENT
AND HEALTH IN GHANA
Esther Yaa. Apewokin

Chapter 8   173
POPULATION AND HEALTH
CARE FACILITIES IN GHANA
Frank Nyonator

Chapter 9   183
CONCLUSION
Stephen O. Kwankye and Chuks J. Mba

vi

About the Contributors

Mrs. Esther Yaa Apewokin is the Executive Director of the National Population Council Secretariat Ghana. She has worked in the Ministry of Finance and Economic Planning in Ghana for 15 years before joining the National Population Council as Director of Programmes, Research and Training. She has written articles on Population Gender and Health, and has attended many conferences in these areas. Mrs. Apewokin holds a Masters Degree in Economics and a Post Graduate Diploma in Development Economics.
Email: apewokinesther@hotmail.com

S. K. Gaisie, Ph.D, is Professor, Regional Institute for Population Studies, University of Ghana, Legon. He is the President of the Population Association of Ghana (PAG). Prof. Gaisie has worked in a number of organizations across Africa. He was the United Nations Chief Technical Adviser to the Statistical Office, Zambia and the University of Zambia. He has worked as the Head, Department of Demography, University of Botswana. Also, he was the Head Population Studies Unit and Director of Population Dynamics Programme at the Institute for Statistical, Social and Economic Research. Prof. Gaisie is an international consultant on population and development interrelationships. He has written a number of books, technical reports, and papers in scholarly journals. Prof. Gaisie holds a PhD degree in Demography from Australia National University, Canberra, as well as M.A degree in Demography from the London School of Economics and Political Science, University of London, and B.A (Hons.) degree in Sociology/Demography from the University College of the Gold Coast.
Email: gaisiesk2002@yahoo.com

Dr. Ing. P. Gyau-Boakye, is a Principal Research Scientist at the Water Research Institute of CSIR, Accra, Ghana. He holds a Ph.D from Ruhr University, Germany, and M.Sc degree from Loughborough University of Technology, UK. He speaks both English and German. He is a Civil Engineer and a member of the Ghana Institution of Engineers.
Email: pgboakye@yahoo.com

Stephen O. Kwankye, Ph.D, is a Senior Lecturer and the immediate past Acting Director of the Regional Institute for Population Studies (RIPS), University of Ghana, Legon. He is also an Associate Project Director of the Population Impact Project (PIP) located at the Department of Geography and Resource Development, University of Ghana, Legon. He is also the Interim General Secretary of the Population Association of Ghana (PAG). Dr. Kwankye's research interests are in Migration, Fertility, Population and Development Interrelationships and Adolescent Sexual and Reproductive Health. He has a number of publications to his credit in his research areas. He holds a BA (Hons.)in Geography with political Science, MA, MPhil and PhD in Population Studies, all from the University of Ghana.
Email: kwankyes@ug.edu.gh

Chuks J. Mba, Ph.D, is Deputy Director/Associate Professor and the Co-ordinator of academic programmes at the Regional Institute for Population Studies, University of Ghana, Legon, Ghana. He is a member of the Steering Committee of the African Research on Ageing Network (AFRAN) and the Deputy General Secretary of Population Association of Ghana (PAG). He is the Coordinator of Thematic Research Network on Reproductive, Maternal and Child Health, and Ageing for the Union for African Population Studies (UAPS). Prof. Mba is a 2002

Laureate of the UAPS Small Grants Program on Population and Development. He has worked in the Civil Service of Nigeria as a Senior Statistician and won a one-year postdoctoral Research Fellowship at the University of Pennsylvania, USA. He has written extensively in peer-reviewed journals, and contributed to reports and book chapters. His research interests include sexual and reproductive health, HIV/AIDS, population ageing, population policies and programmes. Prof. Mba has Ph.D, MPhil, and M.A. degrees in Population Studies from the University of Ghana and B.Sc (Hons.) degree in Statistics from the University of Ilorin, Nigeria. Email: chuksmba@ug.edu.gh

Frank Nyonator, M.D., is the Director of Policy Planning, Monitoring and Evaluation of Ghana Health Service, Accra. Dr. Nyonator is the former Volta Regional Director of Health Administration. He is a member of the Technical Steering Committee of the Child and Adolescent Health (CAH) Department, WHO Headquarters, Geneva. He is also a member of the Global Health Council, American Public Health Association, Population Association of America, and Ghana College of Physicians and Surgeons. Dr. Nyonator has authored and co-authored a number of publications on community-based health planning and services initiative in Ghana, caring for the poor, migration by graduates of the University of Ghana Medical School and others. He has a certificate in Financing Health Care in Developing Countries from Boston University, USA, and a certificate in Health Sector Reform for Primary Health Care from the University of Sussex, Brighton, UK. Furthermore, he has an MPH degree from Leeds University, UK, and MB Ch B degree from the University of Ghana Medical School, Legon. Dr. Nyonator's research interests and experience are in health systems and health service provision.

Emmanuel O. Tawiah, Ph.D, is an Associate Professor and a former Acting Director of the Regional Institute for Population Studies (RIPS), University of Ghana, Legon. He is also an Associate Project Director of the Population Impact Project (PIP), Department of Geography and Resource Development, University of Ghana, Legon and an Executive Member of the Population Association of Ghana (PAG). His research interests include demographic data collection, maternal and child health, household structure and poverty, and adolescent sexual and reproductive health. Prof. Tawiah holds a PhD degree in Sociology/Demography from Duke University, USA, an M.Sc degree in Demography from the University of London, and B.A (Hons.) degree in Sociology from the University of Ghana. Email: etawiah@ug.edu.gh

Acknowledgements

This book is s synthesis of the papers presented during the two-day *Population, Health and Development in Relation to the Millennium Development Goals* Seminar held in Accra in October 2005. It benefited from the generous financial contributions from the UNFPA Ghana, Ghana Health Service, and National Population Council Secretariat. In this respect, we wish to thank Major (Rtd) Courage Quashigah, the Hon. Minister of Health, Dr. Makane Kane, the UNFPA Representative in Ghana, and Mrs Esther Yaa Apewokin, the Executive Director of the National Population Council Secretariat.

The President of PAG, Prof. S.K. Gaisie, spear-headed the campaign to make the publication of this volume possible. His quest for this publication was born out of the fact that as one of Africa's foremost and accomplished demographers, Prof. Gaisie knows that a publication of this sort will stimulate interest in population and development issues, as well as assist in developing a viable relationship with policy makers, programme managers, and opinion leaders, in addition to fostering collaboration among institutions and persons engaged in population and related fields. We therefore say a big "thank you" to him.

A number of other organizations and individuals have also contributed in making the publication of this volume possible. While we do not intend to be exhaustive we gratefully acknowledge the use of the facilities of the Regional Institute for Population Studies (RIPS) to co-ordinate the activities of PAG and especially the seminar which gave birth to the publication of this book. We also express our gratitude to the management and staff of the Coconut Groove Regency Hotel where the seminar was hosted. The efforts of Prof. E.O. Tawiah and other Executive Members of PAG are deeply appreciated. We are thankful for the excellent secretarial services provided by Messrs Becky Atisu, Beatrice Richardson, Leticia Ocloo, and the entire staff of RIPS for their contributions

towards the successful organization of the seminar leading to this publication.

Our profound gratitude goes to Mrs. Akoss Ofori-
Mensah, the Managing Director of Sub-Saharan
Publishers, for her understanding, co-operation and
assistance. She and her professional team worked assid-
uously and meticulously to give this book its beautiful
and state-of-the-art outlook.

We are grateful to all those who presented papers at
the seminar and all the participants. To the others who
have not been mentioned we thank you all for your contribution in making this publication a reality.

C.J. Mba and S.O. Kwankye

Dedication

This book is dedicated to all those individuals and organizations whose interests, research efforts, decisions, policies, and programmes contribute toward the attainment of the Millennium Development Goals.

Preface

The United Nations Population Fund Country Office in Ghana expresses its welcome to this important publication. The areas covered– population growth, adolescent sexual and reproductive health, HIV/AIDS, gender equality and women's empowerment – squarely correspond with the provisions of the International Conference for Population and Development for which the Government of Ghana/UNFPA Fifth Country Programme (2006-2010), is addressing, namely reproductive health, population and development and gender.

A number of key issues have been raised in this book, but it is particularly noteworthy that the authors have paid attention to the intertwined and intractable nature of these problems. The relationship between the health outcome and gender, service delivery and population, are one of the few examples which these analyses have rightly recognized and underlined as critical linkages. It is further emphasized that population issues are central to the achievement of poverty reduction and sustainable development. Fertility decline and its implications for public policy, the demand for water and sanitation, population and health care facilities, to name a few, are the subjects researched into by the members of the Population Association of Ghana, which have implications for the pace and nature of development in Ghana.

The publication of these studies is especially timely, given the consensus made at the 2005 World Summit where world leaders reaffirmed the need to keep reproductive health, HIV/AIDS and gender equality at the top of the development agenda. This renewed high-level commitment is a testimony of the success made through more than a decade of advocacy efforts since the International Conference on Population and Development in Cairo in 1994. Critical contributions made by the research to this process are particularly significant. Ghana, in collaboration with its development partners and the UN system, has an important role to play, not only to maintain the momentum generated by the Summit, but also to further advance the agenda, using research as a tool to strengthen evidence-based advocacy.

Reading through the articles one is strongly reminded that many challenges still remain and that efforts need to be accelerated in order for the country to achieve most of the MDGs by 2015. With the commitment of the government and its partners as well as the ample knowledge produced through such research that provides some answers, I am confident that progress will be made in addressing the bottlenecks and identifying the critical next steps

The Population Association of Ghana had received support from this office to organize a symposium on the research findings. Given the importance of the various contributions, UNFPA is now supporting their publication and dissemination to relevant partners including ministries, research institutions, universities, NGOs, CBOs and media. I am certain that the book will generate meaningful discussions and be used to raise the public awareness and to inform policy and programme formulation, implementation and monitoring.

Makane Kane
UNFPA Representative

14th December 2006

Chapter 1

Introduction

Stephen O. Kwankye and Chuks J. Mba

The Population Association of Ghana (PAG), in line with its aim of furthering the scientific study of population and related activities with a view to improving the quality of life of the people of Ghana, organized a two-day Population Seminar in Accra in collaboration with the Ghana Health Service and the National Population Council Secretariat on 26th – 27th October 2005 on the theme: *Population, Health and Development in Relation to the Millennium Development Goals.* This book is the outcome of the seminar.

A number of papers were presented during the two-day seminar which brought together over 100 participants from the academic, health, civil society and the media to deliberate on key findings of the research papers in relation to the overall drive towards the Millennium Development Goals (MDGs).

The presentations covered issues of population, health, infant and child mortality, sexual and reproductive health of adolescents, HIV/AIDS and survival, water and sanitation, among others. The principal objective of the seminar was to create the platform to engage both researchers, policy makers/implementers and the media in discussions on the critical population and health related issues that should be subjects of concern in order to chart a common cause towards the attainment of the MDGs by 2015.

Dr. Gloria Quansah Asare of the Ghana Health Service chaired the opening session of the Seminar. In her address, she underscored the relevance of the theme of the Seminar for the development of Ghana. According to her, health (preventive and curative) is an issue for all members of the household and therefore should be of concern to everyone. She called on researchers to involve the health sector in their work and re-enforced the commitment of the health sector to such a process of partnership. She expressed the hope that there would be further discussions beyond the presentation of research papers at the Seminar as a way of informing policies towards the attainment of the MDGs.

Prof. S.K. Gaisie, the Interim President of PAG, in his welcome address stressed the relevance of using science to solve problems that afflict the human population of every country. Describing the Seminar as a novelty from a young association such as PAG, he drew attention to the fact that population interacts with all development variables and cautioned that "we cannot postpone action because of ignorance". He therefore called for serious attention to be given to research findings to direct the nation's policy actions, emphasising that functional integration of population into development is what Ghana needs as a country if indeed she wishes to achieve any of the MDGs by the set date.

In her address, Mrs. Esther Apewokin, the Executive Director of the National Population Council (NPC) Secretariat, acknowledged the pool of expertise the membership of PAG has and called on them to use their research findings to assist in addressing population-related problems especially towards poverty reduction as one key component of the MDGs.

In the submission of Mr. Amadu Bawa from the UNFPA Ghana Office, who represented the UNFPA Representative in Ghana, he stressed that one of the main aims of the UNFPA is to ensure that any pregnancy is wanted and women are treated with dignity. He acknowledged that research could be very frustrating due to funding problems. However, one cannot make any development progress by ignoring research. He was therefore glad that the UNFPA was associated with the

Seminar and pledged the support of the UNFPA towards the publication of the Seminar papers to expand their dissemination. The publication of this book is therefore a fulfilment of that pledge for which PAG is very much grateful.

The Minister of Health, Hon. Major (Retd.) Courage Quashiga, gave the keynote address. In presenting his address, the Minister did not hide his commitment to crusading a cause that would lead to a change in the way of doing things in the health sector. He was of the opinion that the population of any nation includes all ages that must be converted into human resource. He noted that of the eight MDGs, three are directly related to health and the other five indirectly.

Quoting from the 1992 Republican Constitution of Ghana, the Minister of Health made it clear that the mandate of his Ministry is to reduce ill-health. He recalled that the Government's approach towards the attainment of middle-income status by the year 2015 is founded on good governance, human resource development and private sector development, the foundation of which, is good health for the population. He cited the case of Israel, which has used the power of the human mind to transform an otherwise dry and sandy desert into a flourishing arable agricultural land. He compared with a note of sadness, the case of Ghana vis-à-vis countries like Malaysia, which at independence (coming three months after Ghana's independence) had a Gross Domestic Product (GDP) of $270.00 (which at the time was behind Ghana's $390.00) and now could boast of a GDP of over $4,000.00 with Ghana's hovering around just $400.00. He attributed Malaysia's economic progress to massive human resource development.

He further explained that the development of the population is dependent on the population and population on development. It is therefore possible to create wealth through improvement in health. Unfortunately, according to him, the nation is producing unemployable graduates leading to what he called an "Association of Unemployed Graduates". There is therefore the need for government to guide people to acquire skills and get adequate training to be useful tools in the nation's development agenda. He expressed concern about how, as a people, we could avoid ill-health, thereby saving resources that otherwise would be used for medical care. The emphasis to him is thus in the area of preventive health care rather than curative.

The Minister of Health further observed that maintaining the health of the population would have to include the maintenance of sanitation, eating nutritious food, etc. Unfortunately, in Ghana, many people eat too much food only to fall sick. He consequently, advised that people should learn to live in healthy accommodation, adopt realistic lifestyles and do regular exercise. He tasked the PAG to explore the possibility of a research that would help determine the level of Intelligence Quotient (IQ) in Ghana.

While expressing his desire for all households to own and make use of insecticide treated bed nets, the Health Minister called on all to endeavour to keep the environment free from mosquitoes otherwise, "we would come out of the bed nets to meet the mosquitoes waiting for us", a situation, which he said would render all our efforts meaningless.

He hoped the papers that were to be presented at the Seminar would bring out policy directions as to how the health issues that are of critical concern would be addressed. While pledging his support to the PAG for organising the Seminar, he called for open-minded discussions that would produce recommendations that are of practical relevance towards the attainment of the MDGs by 2015.

In all ten (10) research papers were presented at the two-day Seminar. The topics covered include fertility trends and implications for public policy, infant and child health, adolescent sexuality and reproductive health, HIV/AIDS and survival challenges, women's empowerment and health, health and nutrition, prenatal care utilisation as a component of maternal and child survival, medical brain drain in developing countries in

Ghana, population, water, sanitation and health. Seven of the papers are published in this volume. Each of the papers published in this volume raises a number of issues that are relevant to policy. They are therefore not just for academic purposes, but go a long way to initiate relevant debates in the various areas of research that have been covered.

Writing on **FERTILITY DECLINE IN GHANA: IMPLICATIONS FOR PUBLIC POLICY** in Chapter 2, S.K. Gaisie contends that after over two decades of high and almost constant fertility, Ghana began experiencing a steady fertility decline since the 1990s. There has since been a gradual move towards fertility transition in the country. In the light of this positive demographic development, this chapter employs a number of estimation procedures and strategies to derive plausible levels of fertility and trends during the period of the transition. The analysis estimates the quantum and pace of the fertility decline and makes a projection to the year 2015, predicting the plausible number of births in a year, the total fertility rate and the number of females of reproductive age during 1960-2015. In addition, it examines the changing age structure during the same period and highlights the inherent policy implications.

It observes among other things that the changing age structures would bring along both development benefits and socio-economic and health problems. The caution however, is that the development benefits of the fertility decline would not be automatic but would depend to a large extent, on effective development policies including the provision of gainful employment to the expanding working age population. It concludes with the message of a restrained hope, which should not be confused with complacency while taking urgent actions to mitigate any gloom or hopelessness that the transition may present in the nation's quest to attain the Millennium Development Goals.

Emmanuel O. Tawiah's paper on **INFANT AND CHILD HEALTH: EVIDENCE FROM 2003 GHANA DEMOGRAPHIC AND HEALTH SURVEY** in Chapter 3 describes infant and child health inequalities in Ghana and examines some relevant factors that affect the treatment of fever/cough and diarrhoea, two common causes of ill-health among children in the country. This is against the backdrop of the fact that the unacceptably high levels of infant, child and under-five mortality in Ghana result in excessive and sheer waste of human lives. Using data from the 2003 Ghana Demographic and Health Survey, he provides an analysis of childhood mortality, vaccination, breastfeeding practices, anthropometric indicators of nutritional status of children, prevalence of anaemia, acute respiratory infection, fever and diarrhoea in children and their treatment, micronutrient intake among children as well as the predictors of receiving medical treatment for diarrhoea and fever/cough.

Among other things, the analysis shows that the Northern Region is the most disadvantaged region, which is mainly the result of the inadequate number of health institutions serving a large population living in a wide range of dispersed settlements. In contrast, the Greater Accra Region is the most advantaged with the lowest proportion of stunted children relative to all the regions.

It concludes that in view of Northern Region's dispersed nature of localities, there is the need for the establishment of more health institutions to serve the health needs particularly those of infants and children in order for the region to catch up with the rest of the country to attain the Millennium Development Goal of reducing under-five mortality by two-thirds by 2015.

Chapter 4, authored by Stephen O. Kwankye, on **ADOLESCENT SEXUALITY AND REPRODUCTIVE HEALTH IN GHANA: SOME RESULTS FROM A SURVEY OF CAPE COAST AND MANKRONG** examines adolescent sexuality and reproductive health in Ghana with evidence from a female adolescent survey of Cape Coast and Mankrong. It also elicits information from focus group discussions carried out separately among adolescents and adults in the two study areas. It basically examines the reproductive health situation by comparing the rural to the urban areas. It has the overall objective of analysing adolescent sexuality with respect to marriage for the purpose of examining the possible reproductive health implications for female adolescents in Ghana.

It examines the age at initiation into sexual activity in the two study areas, investigates the factors that affect sexual initiation and analyses the variations between female adolescents and their sexual partners. It further examines the extent to which marriages among female adolescents are pregnancy-induced, and the reproductive health implications of adolescent sexuality for human capital development.

The analysis uses simple statistical techniques including proportions. Multiple regression analysis is however, employed to examine two main hypotheses namely, "there is an inverse relationship between age at first sexual intercourse and childbearing among female adolescents" and "education relates inversely with childbearing among adolescents". In the analysis, the number of pregnancies ever had is used to discuss childbearing implications instead of actual birth performance.

Major findings include a relatively higher proportion of adolescents ever having sexual intercourse in the rural area compared to the urban. It also shows that for a considerable proportion of ever married female adolescents from either study area, their marriages are pregnancy-induced i.e., they got married after they had been impregnated. There are also suggestions that females become sexually active earlier than males. The analysis confirms the two proposed hypotheses. Financial reasons are shown as one of the major considerations for adolescents to indulge in sex with much older men.

Among other things, it recommends the passage of a law compelling each District Assembly to establish youth recreation and counselling centres for adolescents on their reproductive health in view of the apparent barrier in communication between parents and adolescents on reproductive health issues at home. It also recommends the organization of a national comprehensive study to focus on both male and female adolescents, and calls for a reconciliation between the policy environment and the legal framework regarding adolescent sexual and reproductive health in Ghana.

Writing on **POPULATION GROWTH, WATER/ SANITATION AND HEALTH** in Chapter 5, S. K. Gaisie and P. G. Gyau-Boakye examine the apparent relationship between population growth, water/sanitation and health in Ghana. This is discussed with respect to the observation that population expansion without a corresponding water supply, which is well protected could endanger the health of the human population through the contraction of water-related diseases including notably, diarrhoea, cholera and guinea worm. Based on data from the 1984 and 2000 population censuses of Ghana, it analyses the main sources of water supply for households, solid and liquid waste disposal, access to toilet facility, domestic water supply for the rural and urban areas, and further estimates the future population and water demand levels.

Among other things, the study finds that in the urban areas, the estimated levels of water demand far exceed production and if water production is not substantially increased in the coming years, it is very unlikely that the projected water demand would be met by 2015. This is reinforced by the fact that although the national average for potable water supply in the rural areas increased from 41% to 52% during 1984-1998, it declined to 44% in 2000, a situation, which is attributable mainly to population expansion. The implication is that rapid population expansion would tend to engender severe water sustainability problems, including rapidly increasing water scarcity that would result in the inability of the nation to protect water quality. Consequently, the nation would not be able to avoid water-related infections. It concludes that demographic trends play critical roles in increasing water demand and therefore, policy and decision makers as well as water management specialists urgently need to assess these trends with the aim of integrating them into the development programmes of the country.

In Chapter 6, Chuks J. Mba explores **HIV/AIDS AND**

SURVIVAL CHALLENGES IN SUB-SAHARAN AFRICA: AN ILLUSTRATION WITH GHANA AND SOUTH AFRICA. The HIV continues to spread in Africa and around the world, moving into communities previously little troubled by the epidemic and strengthening its grip on areas where AIDS is already the leading cause of death in adults. Using secondary data from United Nations agencies, this chapter examines current prevalence levels, as well as progress and challenges in efforts to combat HIV/AIDS in Africa.

In four Southern African countries (Botswana, Zimbabwe, Swaziland, and Lesotho), the national adult HIV prevalence rate has risen higher than was thought possible and now exceeds 24 percent. West Africa is relatively less affected by HIV infection, but the prevalence rates in some countries are creeping up. HIV infection in Eastern Africa varies between adult prevalence rates of 4.9 percent in the Democratic Republic of Congo to 15.0 percent in Kenya. The total number of persons infected with HIV has been increasing across the region, overwhelming majority of whom are adults aged 15-49.

This chapter seeks to further raise awareness and expand knowledge about the deleterious effect of HIV/AIDS mortality on Africa's life expectancy by conducting a comparative study of South Africa (with a relatively high HIV/AIDS prevalence rate of 19.9 percent of the total population) and Ghana (with a low prevalence rate – 3.6 percent of the total population). Using the multiple and associated single decrement life table techniques, the study estimates the total number of both South Africans and Ghanaians who would die from HIV/AIDS by the time they reach age 75 from a hypothetical cohort of 100,000 live births, assuming that the mortality conditions of 1996 for (South Africa) and 2000 (for Ghana) prevailed.

The findings presented in this chapter indicate that under the prevailing mortality conditions, 5.7 percent of South African babies and 7.2 percent of Ghanaian babies will eventually die of HIV/AIDS. Furthermore, 7.7 percent and 11.5 percent of South Africans aged 60 years, and 75 years and above respectively, will die of HIV/AIDS. The corresponding figures for Ghana are respectively, 13.0 percent and 23.4 percent. An overwhelming majority of deaths due to AIDS will come from persons within the reproductive and productive age groups in both countries. There is a tremendous gain in life expectancy to the tune of about 26 years (from 63.6 to 89.8 years) for South Africa and 10 years (from 53.3 to 63.0 years) for Ghana that would result in the absence of HIV/AIDS.

In some countries there have been early and sustained prevention efforts. These prevention efforts include less sexual activity, having fewer multiple partners, and more consistent use of condoms. Unfortunately, the high level of HIV/AIDS awareness among the general public has not translated into significant positive behavioural change. Given our traditional extended family system, there should be a strong interest in focusing on the family as a strategy for HIV/AIDS prevention, care, and treatment in Africa. As the disease kills both young and old persons, it is vital that everything is done to bring about a substantial reduction in HIV/AIDS mortality in order to increase Africa's life expectancy.

Writing on **WOMEN'S EMPOWERMENT AND HEALTH IN GHANA** in Chapter 7, Esther Yaa Apewokin brings to the fore the importance of women's health as part of the drive towards achieving overall empowerment of women as a desirous component of Ghana's socio-economic development agenda. Interestingly and rightly so, women's health is attracting much global concern. This is especially the case in sub-Saharan Africa with the advent of HIV/AIDS, which to date, has affected more women than men. Also, considering that in Africa, women are in most cases the primary care givers to the sick and children, the consequences of poor health of women are borne not only by the women themselves but also the entire household, the community and the nation.

The analysis traces the milestones towards the

acknowledgement of the rights of women and children from 1945 to 1994 when the whole world accepted that women in particular, have reproductive and health rights. This was also reinforced at the 1995 Fourth World Conference on Women, which recognised women's rights as human rights. Hitherto, reproductive decisions have been the preserve of men.

The chapter draws attention to the disadvantaged position of most women in household decision-making to the extent that on account of the socio-cultural environment women often find themselves, some of them are unable to make decisions regarding health care for themselves and their children. It further outlines some of the policies and programmes that have been evolved in Ghana to address the challenges in the way of women's empowerment, which it highlights to include the socio-cultural environment, poverty and low education of women. It concludes by allaying the fear particularly of men that empowerment of women does not seek to lower the status of men but rather enhances it. It consequently, calls on all to lend support to policies and programmes towards women's empowerment as envisaged in the Millennium Development Goals.

Chapter 8, which is on **POPULATION AND HEALTH CARE FACILITIES IN GHANA** by Frank Nyonator focuses on health care facilities in Ghana within the context of population growth in the country. It acknowledges that although the health status of the Ghanaian population has improved since independence, the rate of change has been slow with current health indicators far from satisfactory. It therefore discusses the strategic policy direction of the Ghana Health Service (GHS) i.e., the three-tier level of service provision, which has brought about a doubling of the number of health facilities in the country. However, the barriers to health are still not overcome in the face of increasing emigration of health professionals notably doctors and nurses. This situation unfortunately continues to make meaningless the rapid expansion of health facilities that has been achieved throughout the country. The paper also analyses the

11

trend in antenatal, supervised delivery and family planning coverage during 2000-2004 and concludes that most of the health facilities are under-utilized. This is explained to be due to the fact that majority of people living in communities do not want sophisticated clinics and hospitals but someone who is nearby to provide the required professional direction as to what to do in times of ill-health. It therefore recommends among other things, that priority should be given to building community level facilities that are envisaged to go a long way to serve the growing population better in order to achieve the country's Millennium Development Goals in the area of health care delivery.

It is hoped that the findings and issues raised in the papers published in this volume would provide the opportunity for further discussions beyond the scope of this publication. It should also present avenues for increased collaborative multi-disciplinary research in addition to providing platforms for continued debate until answers are found to the developmental problems that these studies have so far unearthed.

Chapter 2

Fertility Decline in Ghana: Implications for Public Policy

S. K. Gaisie

Introduction

The population of Ghana has undergone a structural transformation since the beginning of the fertility decline in the late 1980s. Accompanying the decline are a number of issues that need to be investigated or researched into in order to assess their demographic, social, political and economic impact.

Sample surveys (i.e. 1960 Post-Enumeration Survey, 1968/69 Demographic Sample Survey and 1971 Supplementary Inquiry) provided the information required for determination of the level of fertility in the 1960s and 1970s. All the estimates of the total fertility rates indicated that the country's fertility was high and stable, lying in the neighbourhood of between 6.7 and 7 children per woman. A total fertility rate of 6.9 children per woman appeared to be the most plausible estimate (Gaisie, 1969; 1974; Gaisie and deGraft Johnson, 1976).

Estimates based on the 1979/1980 Ghana Fertility Survey (GHS) data indicate that total fertility rate for the period 1960s to mid-1970s ranged between 6.85 and 6.99 children per woman. Evaluation and adjustment of the data for the recent period (1975-1980) yielded a total fertility rate of 6.69 as compared with the reported one of 6.47 (Gaisie, 2005).

All told, the estimates derived from the data sets spanning a period of more than 25 years show that the level of fertility was high and stable during the 1960s, 1970s and early 1980s. The reported total fertility rates derived from the 1993, 1998 and 2003 Demographic and Health Surveys data indicate a significant and steady fertility decline since then; falling from 6.43 in 1988 to 5.50 in 1993, 4.55 in 1998 and then to 4.44 in 2003.

However, the need to detect and measure trends in fertility with accuracy and sensitivity in a society that is experiencing population expansion is crucial for competent planning. For instance, plausible fertility estimates based on reliable data are critical for construction of population projections as well as for monitoring and evaluating action programmes for reducing the rate of growth via family limitation. A number of estimation procedures and strategies were therefore employed to derive plausible estimates of fertility levels and trends during the transition period. The results are presented elsewhere (Gaisie, 2005). Substantive issues and their implications are the subject-matter of this chapter.

Quantum and Pace of Decline

Three estimation procedures yielded estimates which suggest that the level of fertility in Ghana fell from about seven children per woman in the 1960s and 1970s to 4.6 children per woman by the turn of the last century; a decline of 33% during the 43 year period (1960-2000) or an annual decline of 0.8% as depicted in Figure 1. The average number of children born to a Ghanaian woman was reduced by 2.3 children; a reduction of 0.05 children per year during the entire period. The pace of the decline, however, increased to 0.2 children per year during the late 1980s and the 1990s and slowed down considerably to 0.04 children per year by the beginning of the 21st century with the total fertility rate falling from 4.8 in the late 1990s to 4.6. The change was much more marked among the younger women (20-35-year olds) than among the older cohorts, particularly during the second half of the 1990s. However, the decline appears to have stalled.

Figure 1. Total Fertility Rate: 1960-2003

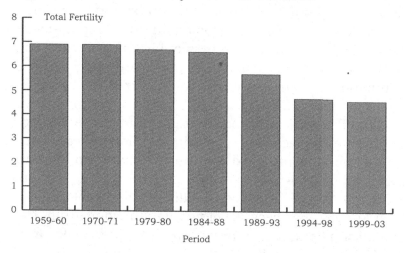

Fertility Decline and High Rate of Growth

Fertility trends affect the rate of growth by determining the number of births women have, and the size of the different generations. In a majority of the African countries where fertility is above replacement level, children outnumber their parents by substantial amounts and the children in turn have more children than required to replace their parents' generations even when fertility level is declining (Table1). Consequently, as fertility falls, the number of births to relatively large generations of parents is higher for some time than the number of deaths in the population, most of which are that of grand parents and great grand-parents. This process tends to maintain a relatively high positive population growth rate even though fertility is falling. In most of the countries where fertility rate is reported to be falling, overall population growth rates are relatively high, implying that fertility rate is still high and in consequence the balancing of the demographic "deficit" will take sometime to be effected.

This is exactly what is happening in Ghana at the moment. Population continues to grow after fertility reaches replacement level[1] because of a temporary imbalance in the age structure. When fertility declines from high to low levels, populations tend to be characterized (for about 15 to 20 years later) by unusually large proportions of men and women in their reproductive years, leading to large numbers of births even when fertility rates are low. This is an important aspect of the population age structure which is referred to as "population momentum".

It has been estimated that an immediate fertility decline to replacement level in developing countries would be accompanied by an ultimate population increase of two-thirds before growth ceased (Keyfitz 1971:83-89) For instance, Japan reached replacement level in 1957, but because of population momentum, the Japanese population is projected to keep growing until 2006. Hence, even if Ghana's fertility reaches replacement level in 2050, the population will continue to grow for a considerable length of time during the course of the 21st century.

Table 1 Births, Total Fertility Rate and Females Aged 15-49 Years 1960-2015

Births Per:	1960	2000	2005	2015
Year	350,000	640,000	673,000	697,000
Day	958	1,793	1,844	1,910
Total Fertility Rate	6.9	4.7	4.6	4.4
Females aged 15-49 [millions]	1.4	4.5	5.1	6.5

Changing Age Structures

The age structure of Ghana in 2000 is typical of a country just entering the demographic transition from high to low fertility. There is a broad base at the bottom consisting of large number of children and a narrow top with relatively small number of elderly. Though the proportion under 15 years is decreasing as a result of fertility decline, it is still relatively high (Figure 2); the decline has not as yet had any significant effect on that segment of the population and the dependency burden is still heavy and "demographic bonus" is yet to be realised[2].

Figure 2 Proportion Under 15 Years of Age, 1960-2015

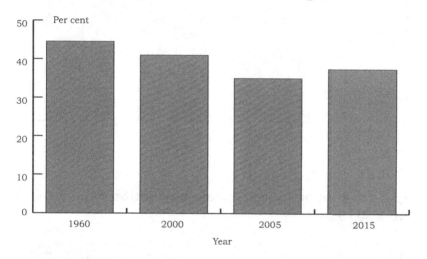

The female population aged 15-49 years increased from 1.4 million in 1960 to 1.9 million, 2.8 million and 4.5 million in 1970, 1984 and 2000 respectively and it is expected to climb up to 6.5 million in 2015 (Figure 3). The number of births per year increased from 345,000 in 1960-1965 to 640,000 per year in 2000-2005 and it is expected to increase to 697,000 in 2010-2015. Thus, large number of births and the size of different generations will generate expansion of the population even though fertility has been declining.

The proportion of the female population increased from 42% in 1960 to 48% in 2005 and it is estimated to rise to 50 per cent within the next decade (Figure 4); a clear indication of occurrence of large numbers of births and high growth potential inherent in the age structure. The substantial increase in the number of females of the childbearing age range over the years also puts pressure on expansion of sexual and reproductive health facilities and services.

Figure 3. Females Aged 15-49 Years , 1960-2015

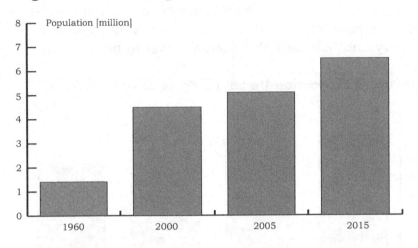

Figure 4. Proportion of Female Population Aged 15-49 1960-2015

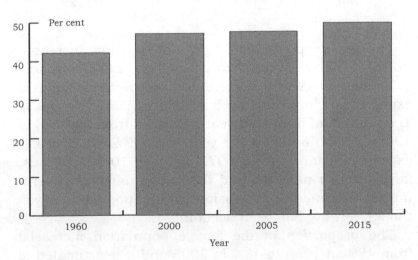

The population of adolescents and young adults (15-24 year-olds) increased from 1.1 million in 1960 to 3.5 million in 2000 and it is estimated to rise to 5.1 million in 2005 and 5.9 million in 2015 (Figure 5). The projected figures indicate that the youthfulness of the population will persist for a considerable length of time, leading to rapid expansion of the population.

In fact, the size of the population of the youth (i.e. persons aged 15-24 years) increased more than three-folds between 1960 and 2000. The rapid growth of the adolescent and youth population exerts increased pressure to expand education and health services and employment opportunities. Medium population projections constructed by the author indicate that the population of the adolescents and young adults will expand for a considerable length of time. Policy and decision-makers must bear this in mind.

In addition to absolute numbers, the proportion of young people in the total population raises policy concerns. The proportion increased from 19% in 1960 to nearly 21.4% in 2000 and it is estimated to climb up to 21.7% in 2010 (Figure 6). A situation in which 20% or more of a population is aged 15-24 years has been described as "Young Bulge". There is a speculation that this phenomenon may subject a society to potentially disruptive, political and social movements.

In addition to increasing services and facilities to cope with large numbers of young people, the expansion of this segment of the population raises two important policy concerns. First, the adolescents and young adults are about to enter or are already in their prime reproductive years, leading to large numbers of births, even when fertility is low. Secondly, adolescents and young adults are prone, among other things, to high-risk sexual behaviour leading to increase in prevalence of HIV/AIDS.

Figure 5 Population Aged 15-24 years [Adolescents and Young Adults] 1960-2015

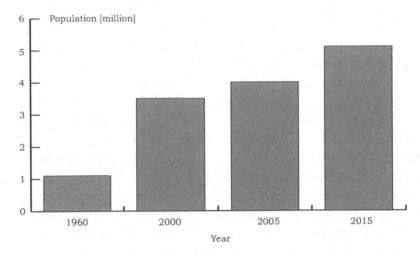

Figure 6. Proportion Aged 15-24 Years, 1960-2015

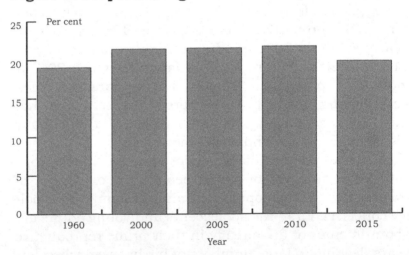

A review of the studies conducted on adolescent sexual and reproductive health highlights the need to systematically investigate the risk and protective behaviours of Ghanaian adolescents in order to assemble research-based evidence for designing strategies for meeting the sexual and reproductive health needs of the youth. Among the key findings is the yawning gap between policies and their translation into programmes and activities

(Awusubo-Asare et. al., 2004). Sexual and contraceptive behaviour of the youth is reported to be influenced in important ways by myriad of factors operating at the individual, family, community and societal levels.

As fertility declines, the proportions in the age groups change. Proportion of young dependents (i.e. under 15-year-olds) drops (Figure 2) while proportions of adolescents and young adults (Figure 3) and old dependents (Figure 7) increase. The proportion aged 65 years and over increased from 2.7% in 1960 to 4.6% in 2000 and it is estimated to rise to 4.9% and 5.3% in 2015 and 2025 respectively.

Ageing may appear to be gradual at the moment but the older population will grow rapidly as the fertility transition advances; depending, of course on the speed of the decline. It will be a great mistake to dismiss aging as an issue that need not be considered until some time in the future. Policy options for this segment of the population will include enhancement of traditional support systems, greater employment opportunities for the elderly who are still capable to remain in the work force, institutions that support high levels of personal savings and government programmes such as pension schemes and health care systems.

Figure 7 Proportion Aged 65 Year and over 1960-2025

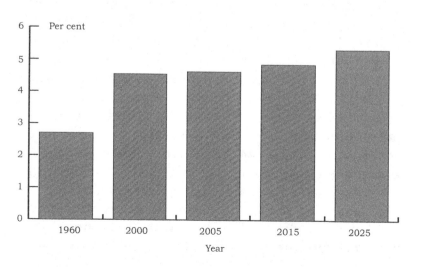

Fertility and Family Planning

There is a huge discrepancy between contraceptive use and the level of fertility. The findings of the 1998 and 2003 Ghana Demographic and Health Surveys show that contraceptive prevalence levels increased from 22% for any method and 13% for any modern method during the mid 1990s to 25% and 19% respectively by the turn of the last century (Ghana Statistical Service/Macro Inc. 1999; 2004). Significant drops in the level of fertility without marked increases in contraceptive prevalence can only be explained in terms of major changes in the proximate determinants - e.g. timing of marriage, commencement of exposure to the risk of childbearing and changes in the durations of postpartum abstinence, amenorrhoea and breastfeeding and foetal losses.

The decomposition of the effect of the proximate determinants of fertility over the past decade (i.e. 1988-1998) indicates that postpartum non-susceptibility (i.e. durations of breastfeeding, postpartum abstinence and amenorrhoea) contributes between 70% and 80% of the total number of births per woman averted by all proximate determinants[3] during the period 1988-1998. The contribution of *marriage* increased slightly from 12% to 14% and that of contraception from 7% to 18%. Put in another way, out of the 7.8 births per woman averted in 1998, 5.5 are attributable to postpartum non-susceptibility variables and only 1.4 births are due to contraceptive use. The contribution of contraception, however, rose from 0.57 births in 1988 to 1.4 in 1993. Thus the effect of contraception appears to have stagnated during the period 1993-1998. The major determinants of the fertility decline are therefore the durations of amenorrhoea, breastfeeding and postpartum abstinence. Abortion may play a very significant role in the fertility transition but lack of information makes it extremely difficult to estimate the extent of its contribution.

To complete the fertility transition, contraceptive prevalence needs to be substantially stepped up. Experience indicates that replacement levels are usually not attained with contraceptive prevalence of less than 50%; levels of 70% are more common among populations with very low fertility. High levels of modern contraceptive use are therefore required for a population to reach replacement level.

Slow Down of the Pace of Decline

Ghana is classified as a medium- or intermediate-fertility country. Intermediate fertility countries are countries that are experiencing fertility decline but the level of fertility is still above replacement level (i.e. 2.1 children per woman). The level of fertility in these countries is estimated to reach replacement level by 2050 (United Nations, 2003).

Replacement level-fertility is a theoretical construct. No population has a built-in replacement mechanism; the replacement fertility-level varies with level of mortality prevalent in the population. Because fertility declines have occurred in many different situations, it is not easy to determine how long it will take a country like Ghana to reach replacement level.

Experience shows that there tends to be a slowdown of the rate of decline during the movement through the transition. Argentina, Uruguay, Egypt and Tunisia, to name a few, have experienced slowdowns during 1950-2000 and they have not yet shown signs of reaching the replacement level. In the case of Tunisia, Stamm and Tsui observed that: "Though fertility declined as a result of technological and economic change, the strength of the traditional and cultural value of the family has prevented the realization of a completed fertility transition" (Stamm and Tsui 1986:159-197).

Recent estimates indicate that the transition will be completed by 2005, more than twenty five years since Tunisia began to experience significant drop in the level of fertility. The total fertility rate of four children per woman remained constant for a considerable length of time before resuming a downward trend. Similar observation has been made in respect of fertility decline in

Egypt: "Relatively steep falls occurred in the 1960s and by the end of the 1970s the crude birth rate was around 37 live births per thousand population. Thereafter, fertility apparently began to stabilize again. The subsequent levelling off is harder to explain" (Caldwell, 1977: 594). Argentina and Uruguay have exhibited similar patterns of fertility. Fertility level dropped to about three children per woman in 1950-1955, but it has remained consistently above replacement level for over forty-five years.

Policy Implications

Fertility and Family Planning

The pace of change has virtually stalled; total fertility now lies in the neighbourhood of between 4.6 and 4.7 children per woman. The question is how quickly will the country reach replacement-level fertility. The answer has enormous implications for the ultimate population size and potential strains on infrastructure, natural resources and the environment. The experience of other countries such as Tunisia and Egypt indicates that cultural and religious props might delay the transition for a considerable length of time. Of the 81 countries in the world that had total fertility rate of 4.5 children per woman or higher in 1960, only six managed to bring the number of births down to two or less per woman by 1990.

The effect of the delayed fertility decline on the ultimate population size is reflected by the population momentum, which generates continued population growth for many years after replacement level. The longer the delay, the more persistent will be the ensuing demographic, economic and social problems. In other words, the longer it takes to complete the transition, the greater the demographic, social and economic impact.

There is therefore an urgent need to step up contraceptive prevalence. High levels of use of effective modern contraceptive methods are required to bring fertility down to tolerable levels. In Asia, six countries which reached replacement levels within a period of 30 years, prevalence rates for modern contraceptive use ranged from 52% in Indonesia to 74% in Taiwan. Five of these countries established national family planning programmes that were arguably the best managed in the world (East-West Centre, 2002). The exceedingly Low levels of contraceptive use in most African countries have been attributed, among other things, to: lack of political will and commitment and dynamic programme leadership at all levels; non-participation in the development process by the bulk of the civil society; and lack of mastery of the methodology of integrating population variables into development planning (ECA, 1995).

An assessment of the performance so far indicates that Ghana has to do more to uplift majority of the people from wretched poverty. The implementation of the family planning programmes has been going on for 35 years, longer than the period taken by some of the East Asian countries to complete the fertility transition. Some progress has been made; fertility has been declining but the country is not out of the woods yet.

To improve the country's performance in tackling the population issues and meet the targets set in the population policy (or in the Millennium Development Goals), the policies and strategies need to be revisited. To remove the constraint noted above, will require alternative or modified strategies.

Changing Age Structures
The changing age structures will bring along development benefits as well as social, economic and health problems. Changes in the age structure bestow special opportunities for rapid economic growth. For instance, expansion of the potential labour force (e.g. changes in the size of the working-age population relative to the dependent populations); changes in the age structure that bolsters saving and investment, and changes in the age structure that promote greater investment in human resources. The development benefits of the fertility decline are not automatic; it will depend, to a large extent, on the effective development policies. For instance, policies relating to provision of gainful employ-

ment to the expanding working-age population; sound and stable macro-economic policies and development of viable financial institutions.

On the other hand, the expanding labour force, the burgeoning youth population (i.e. 15-24 years age group) and the rising elderly population (65 years and over age group) create a number of social, economic and health problems. For instance, the young bulge (15-24 years age group) raises a number of policy concerns including: sexual risk – unwanted pregnancy, spread of HIV and other STIs; impact of school enrolment on the education system; increasing pressure on expansion of health services; employment opportunities; and criminality, smoking and drug abuse.

There is the need to revisit health policies, strategies and programmes to meet the requirements of the burgeoning population group [adolescents and young adults] including the females at the childbearing ages.

The expanding elderly population also raises policy concerns: viability of Traditional (family) support systems; greater employment opportunities; pension schemes; and health care systems.

The demographic realities outlined above, have placed the country in a situation that has given rise to new questions and requirements. For instance, is Ghana going to go through the experience of Tunisia? If so, how long is she going to creep over the *four-child* plateau; bearing in mind the power of traditional and religious props? What are the forces driving fertility through the transition? Can significant drops in the levels of fertility and infant and child mortality occur without equal access to health and education facilities and services, the key to rapid economic growth and efficient poverty reduction? A search for the answers calls for a number of empirical studies that will be required to provide the basis for designing context specific development strategies.

A lot can be achieved by getting the message out that functional integration of population and development is the best strategy for: maximizing population and development achievements; maximizing the capacity building

of the grassroots communities; maximizing their participation in the ongoing political, social and economic and
demographic processes; maximizing the value of knowledge; and maximizing human mind and spirit.

Fortunately, the family planning and other related
programmes are being implemented within a decentralized system. And look at what decentralized system has
done for village communities in other parts of the world;
building their capacities for effective participation in
local development programmes. No other system in the
world has the ability to turn illiterate villagers into imple-
menters of modern development programmes. How can
Ghana take advantage of this development model to
achieve its demographic goals?

The problems posed by population are daunting but
not insuperable. Experience in other countries shows that
dramatic improvements can be achieved, provided the will
and resources are available. The message that should be
sent out therefore is not one of unmitigated gloom or
hopelessness. Rather, it should be one of restrained hope;
of course, not to be confused with complacency. The problems are serious, and urgent action is needed.

References

Awusabo-Asare, K. et. al., 2004. "Adolescent Sexual and
Reproductive Health in Ghana: A Synthesis of Research
Evidence". NEED MAP, *Occasional Report.*

Caldwell, Pat. 1977. "Egypt and Arab and Islamic Worlds" in J.
C. Caldwell (ed.), *Persistence of High Fertility*, Canberra.

Census Office, 1961. *The 1960 Population Census, Volume
V1,The Post-Enumeration Survey* (PES), Accra, Ghana.

Census Office , 1971. The 1970 Population Census,
Supplementary Enquiry (SE), Accra, Ghana.

Central Bureau of Statistics and World Fertility Survey, 1983.
*Ghana Fertility Survey Report 1979/1980, First Report,
Volume 1, Background, Methodology and Findings,*
Accra, Ghana.

Gaisie, S. K. 1969. "Dynamics of Population Growth in Ghana", *Ghana Population Studies No. 1*, Ghana Publishing Corporation (Printing Division), Accra-Tema.

Gaisie, S. K.1974. "Estimating Ghanaian Fertility, Mortality, and Age Structure", *Ghana Population Series No. 6*. Population Dynamics Programme, University of Ghana and
University of North Calorina.

Gaisie, S. K. and de Graft-Johnson, K. T. 1976. *The Population of Ghana*, CICRED, Imprimerie-Louis-Jean, Paris.

Gaisie, S. K. 2005. "Fertility Trend in Ghana" in *African Population Studies*, Vol. 2, October.

Ghana Statistical Service, 2004. *Ghana Population Prospects, 2000-2025*, (Forthcoming), Accra.

Ghana Statistical Service & Macro Inc. 1989. *1988 Demographic and Health Survey Report*, Accra, Ghana & Calverton, Maryland, USA.

Ghana Statistical Service & Macro Inc. 1994   .   *1993 Demographic and Health Survey Report*, Accra, Ghana & Calverton, Maryland, USA.

Ghana Statistical Service & Macro Inc. 1999. *1998 Demographic and Health Survey Report*, Accra , Ghana & Calverton, Maryland, USA.

Ghana Statistical Service & Macro Inc. 2004. *2003 Demographic and Health Survey Report*, Accra, Ghana & Calverton, Maryland, USA.

Keyfitz, N. 1971. "The Impact of Modernization" in *Approaches to the Science of Socio-economic Development*, Paris.

Stamm, L. and Tsui, A. O. 1986. "Cultural Constraints on Fertility Transition in
Tunisia: A case Analysis from the City of Kaar-Hallal" in *Culture and Reproduction: An Anthropological Critique of Demographic Transition Theory* (ed). Peenhandwerker.

United Nations, 2003. *World Population Prospects, The 2002 Revision*, Volume 1, United Nations, New York.

United Nations, 2004. *World Population Prospects, The 2003 Revision, Volume 1*, United Nations, New York.

Chapter 3

Infant and Child Health: Evidence from 2003 Ghana Demographic and Health Survey

Emmanuel O. Tawiah

Introduction

The unacceptably high levels of infant, child and under-five mortality in Ghana result in excessive and sheer waste of human lives. The recent increase in the under-five mortality rate from 107.6 per 1,000 live births during 1994-1998 to 111 per 1,000 live births in the period 1998-2003 makes the achievement of the Millennium Development Goal (MDG) of reducing under-five mortality by two-thirds between 1990 and 2015 quite difficult to attain. Most of these deaths are preventable through the adoption of relatively simple and inexpensive strategies such as breastfeeding promotion, childhood vaccination, provision of basic hygiene and health education.

The factors associated with high infant and child mortality include poverty, malnutrition, poor sanitation and inadequacy of health facilities. In addition, human immunodeficiency virus (HIV) can be transmitted from mother to child before or during child birth and young children whose mothers die are at a very high risk of dying themselves at young age (United Nations, 1994).

The health of infants and children is of crucial importance, both as a reflection of current health status of a large segment of the population and as a predictor of the health of the next generation. In 2000, persons aged less than five years comprised 14.7 % of the total population of Ghana. Protecting the health of this large population of infants and children today is an investment in the labour force of tomorrow. Good infant and child health is synonymous with wealth of the future.

This chapter attempts to describe infant and child health inequalities as well as examine some of the factors that affect treatment of two common causes of ill-health among children namely; fever/cough and diarrhoea.

Methodology

The data are derived from the 2003 Ghana Demographic and Health Survey (GDHS), a nationally representative sample of women aged 15-49. The GDHS was designed to, among other things, collect information from female respondents, who were asked questions on topics such as respondent's background, reproduction, antenatal and delivery care, breastfeeding, immunization, health and nutrition.

The analysis is restricted to women aged 15-49 and their births in the five years preceding the survey. A total of 3,340 births comprising 1,114 or 33.4% and 2,226 or 66.6% respectively in the urban and rural areas were recorded in the five years prior to the survey.

The indicators of infant and child health include breastfeeding practices, vaccination coverage, nutritional status, receipt of vitamin A supplement, prevalence of anaemia, prevalence and treatment of common childhood illnesses such as acute respiratory infection (AR1), fever and diarrhoea. The analysis does not include antenatal, delivery and postnatal care although these activities promote positive infant and child health outcomes.

Two separate analyses are done. Bivariate analyses are used to examine relationships between selected demographic and socio-economic variables and childhood immunization coverage, breastfeeding practices, nutritional status, prevalence of anaemia, receipt of vitamin A supplement, prevalence and treatment-seeking for AR1, fever and diarrhoea. For the logistic regression analysis, all variables are categorical or grouped and for each variable, one category is selected as the reference category (RC). The two dependent variables used in the logistic regression analysis are receipt of medical treatment for fever/cough and receipt of medical treatment for diarrhoea. The results of logistic regression analysis are given as regression coefficients, odds ratio (if greater than unity, the probability of receiving medical treatment is higher than that of non-receipt), and p values, to assess the relative statistical significance of the selected variables.

Results

Childhood Mortality

Poor infant and child health tends to result in high infant and child mortality levels. Table 1 provides information on early childhood mortality in Ghana to serve as a backdrop to examination of infant and child health inequalities by sex, type of place of residence and region. Under-five mortality is relatively high in Ghana. One out of nine children dies before attaining age five. Rural areas have considerably and consistently higher mortality levels than urban areas. For instance, under-five mortality in rural areas is 27% higher than it is in urban areas. There are wide regional differentials in under-five mortality. Under-five mortality varies from 75 per 1,000 live births in the Greater Accra Region to 208 per 1,000 live births in the Upper West Region. The rate for the Upper West region is 2.8 times that of Greater Accra Region and points to the monumental health challenge faced by the former region in her quest to attain the Millennium Development Goal of reducing the under-five mortality rate by two-thirds between 1990 and 2015.

Table 1 Early childhood mortality rates by type of place of residence and region, Ghana 2003

Characteristic	Neonatal mortality	Postneonatal mortality*	Infant mortality	Child mortality	Under-five mortality
Type of place of residence					
Urban	38	17	55	40	93
Rural	43	27	70	52	118
Region					
Western	37	30	66	46	109
Central	(37)	(13)	(50)	(41)	(90)
Greater Accra	29	16	45	31	75
Volta	44	31	75	41	113
Eastern	42	22	64	33	95
Ashanti	57	22	80	40	116
Brong Ahafo	36	22	58	35	91
Northern	38	32	69	90	154
Upper East	22	11	33	48	79
Upper West	62	43	105	115	208
Total	43	21	64	50	111

Note: Rates based on 250 to 499 exposed persons are in brackets.
*Computed as the difference between the infant and neonatal mortality rates.
Source: Ghana Statistical Service, Noguchi Memorial Institute for Medical Research and ORC Macro. 2004, p.129.

Childhood Vaccination

Childhood vaccination remains an important strategy for the reduction of morbidity and mortality from common vaccine-preventable diseases such as tuberculosis, diphtheria, pertussis (whooping cough), tetanus, poliomyelitis and measles. High vaccination coverage is a crucial goal of all child survival programmes in Ghana. The expanded programme on immunization (EPI) of the Ministry of Health follows the World Health Organization (WHO) and United Nations Children's Fund guidelines which recommend that all children receive one dose each of Bacillus Calmette-Guérin (BCG) and measles vaccine, three doses of Diptheria, Polio and Tetanus (DPT) vaccine for the prevention of diptheria, pertussis and tetanus, and three doses of polio vaccine.

In the GDHS, information on vaccination status was collected from health cards, shown to the interviewer and from the mother's verbal reports if no card was available. Information on vaccination coverage among children aged 12-23 months is shown in Table 2. Health cards were presented for 83% of the children aged 12-23 months. Sixty nine per cent of children aged 12-23 months have been fully vaccinated, while 4.8% have received no vaccinations. Boys are slightly more likely to be fully immunised than girls. Immunization coverage is more in urban than rural areas. Apart from the Northern Region where less than half of the children are fully immunized, at least three out of five children in each of the other regions are fully immunised. In both Volta and Central Regions, four in five children are fully immunised.

Ninety one percent of children have received the BCG and first dose of DPT vaccine. Vaccination coverage for both BCG and DPT1 was highest in the Upper East Region and lowest in the Northern Region. Whereas the coverage for the first doses of DPT and polio is high, the dropout rate is also high for DPT3 and polio 3. The dropout rates are 12.4% and 14.8% for DPT and polio respectively. With regard to measles vaccination, it is noted that children in the Northern and Western Regions are particularly disadvantaged, whereas in the other regions at least, four out of five children have received measles vaccine.

Breastfeeding Practices

Infant feeding has an effect on the health of both the child and the mother. Feeding practices are important determinants of children's nutritional status and many studies have shown the beneficial effects of breastfeeding on the nutritional status, morbidity and mortality of young infants (Shah and Khanna, 1990; Ahiadeke, 2003). Mothers were asked about the current breastfeeding status of all children under five years of age and, if the child was being breastfed, whether other liquid or complementary solid foods were given to the child during the 24 hours before the survey.

Table 2   Percentage of children 12-23 months who had received specific vaccines by the time of the survey and the percentage with a vaccination card according to child's sex, type of place of residence and region, Ghana 2003

Characteristic		Percentage of children who received										Percentage with vaccination card	Number of children
	BCG	DPT			Polio*				Measles	All**	None		
		DPT1	DPT2	DPT3	Polio 0	Polio 1	Polio 2	Polio 3					
Male	92.5	91.6	87.3	81.3	50.9	93.8	89.7	80.4	83.2	70.3	4.3	84.9	375
Female	89.5	90.0	85.6	77.3	57.0	92.0	87.6	77.7	83.2	68.2	5.4	80.7	321
Type of place of residence													
Urban	95.9	94.0	91.5	86.2	77.6	95.1	91.4	82.8	85.8	77.5	3.3	84.6	248
Rural	88.5	89.1	83.7	75.8	40.4	91.8	87.3	77.1	81.8	66.0	5.6	82.0	447
Region													
Western	92.5	91.1	86.7	78.9	44.3	95.7	93.2	83.7	76.4	60.4	4.3	87.4	59
Central	95.2	95.2	92.6	87.9	25.5	95.2	95.2	89.0	86.5	82.1	2.6	84.0	68
Greater Accra	91.0	91.4	84.5	78.7	81.7	90.3	87.0	77.4	87.8	69.1	4.5	82.6	75
Volta	91.2	95.6	91.4	89.3	47.5	95.6	91.4	90.3	89.4	82.3	4.4	85.5	66
Eastern	88.8	91.8	82.5	77.0	57.0	89.9	79.5	73.1	79.1	65.6	8.2	84.8	77
Ashanti	92.8	91.7	90.7	82.4	60.0	94.5	89.8	79.7	82.2	71.6	5.5	76.5	123
Brong Ahafo	91.1	91.5	89.5	85.3	70.0	94.0	91.7	83.4	87.1	79.0	4.5	87.5	75
Northern	84.1	77.9	70.0	62.2	48.6	87.3	81.4	62.5	76.0	48.0	5.1	80.9	92
Upper East	97.8	99.1	97.8	77.8	30.0	97.8	95.0	84.1	91.2	77.0	0.9	87.9	39
Upper West	91.4	89.7	87.8	75.5	49.9	93.0	89.9	74.1	79.5	60.3	7.0	75.6	21
Total	91.1	90.8	86.5	79.5	53.7	93.0	88.7	79.2	83.2	69.4	4.8	83.0	698

Table 3 presents information on the median duration of any breastfeeding, exclusive breastfeeding and predominant breastfeeding among children born in the three years before the survey by sex, type of place of residence and region. The median duration of any breastfeeding is 22.5 months, while exclusive breastfeeding defined as receiving breast milk only for the first six months of life and predominant breastfeeding are 2.3

Table 3 Median duration of any breastfeeding, exclusive breastfeeding and predominant breastfeeding among children born in the three years preceding the survey by sex, type of place of residence and region, Ghana 2003

Characteristic	Median duration (months) of breastfeeding			Number of children
	Any breastfeeding	Exclusive breastfeeding	Predominant breastfeeding[1]	
Sex				
Male	22.8	2.8	5.1	168
Female	22.3	1.2	5.1	143
Type of place of residence				
Urban	20.4	4.1	5.0	97
Rural	23.3	1.4	5.1	214
Region				
Western	20.2	0.6	2.4	34
Central	21.3	0.5	6.3	22
Greater Accra	19.3	5.7	6.9	28
Volta	22.9	3.2	4.1	27
Eastern	21.2	2.9	3.4	23
Ashanti	20.6	1.9	3.2	59
Brong Ahafo	22.6	3.5	6.2	39
Northern	28.2	0.7	7.4	47
Upper East	26.4	1.4	8.3	20
Upper West	27.4	5.1	7.0	13
Total	22.5	2.3	6.9	312

Note: Median durations are based on current status.
1. Either exclusively breastfed or received breast milk and plain water, water-based liquids, and/or juice only (excludes other milk).

months and 6.9 months respectively. Regional differences in breastfeeding prevalence are minimal, with the
longest duration of 28 months being in the Northern
Region, while the lowest duration is reported for Greater
Accra Region (19.3 months). The median duration of 2.3
months of exclusive breastfeeding falls short of
WHO/UNICEF recommendation of exclusive breastfeeding for the first six months of life.

Anthropometric Indicators of Nutritional Status of Children

The importance of good nutrition in the growth and
development of infants and children can hardly be
overemphasized. The 2003 GDHS collected anthropometric data for all children who were born in the five
years preceding the survey. The anthropometric data
allow objective measurement and evaluation of the nutritional status of young children. Three standard indices
of physical growth namely; height-for-age (stunting),
weight-for-height (wasting) and weight-for-age (underweight) are used to assess the nutritional status of children. Table 4 shows the percentage of children under
five years classified as malnourished according to
height-for-age, weight-for-height and weight-for-age by
sex, type of place of residence and region. The analysis is
restricted to 3,183 (89%) out of 3,586 children under five
years identified in the household because of missing
information, implausibly high or low values and incomplete age information.

Overall, 30% of children are stunted and 11% are
severely stunted. Seven per cent of children are wasted,
while 22% are under weight. Boys are more likely than girls
to be stunted and children in the rural areas are more
stunted than urban children. Regional variation in nutritional status of children is wide. The proportion of children
under five years who are stunted ranges from 13.9% in
Greater Accra Region to 48.8% in the Northern Region. The
Central, Northern, Upper East and Upper West Regions

Table 4 Percentage of children under-five years classified as malnourished according to three anthropometric indices of nutritional status: height for age, weight-for-age, weight-for-height and weight-for-age by sex, type of place of residence and region, Ghana 2003

Characteristic	Height-for-age		Weight-for-height		Weight-for-age		
	Percentage below -3SD	Percentage below -2SD*	Percentage below -3SD	Percentage below -2SD*	Percentage below -3SD	Percentage below -2SD*	Number of children
Sex							
Male	12.5	32.8	1.7	7.2	4.9	22.6	1,588
Female	9.2	27.0	1.0	7.1	4.5	21.6	1,595
Type of place of residence							
Urban	6.8	20.8	1.9	6.6	3.2	15.4	1,050
Rural	12.8	34.5	1.1	7.4	5.4	25.4	2,132
Region							
Western	8.0	28.4	1.1	5.3	2.2	16.5	333
Central	12.5	31.6	0.0	3.0	4.0	22.0	284
Greater Accra	5.5	13.9	2.7	7.2	2.1	11.5	337
Volta	7.8	23.3	3.1	13.9	4.9	25.7	259
Eastern	6.2	27.4	0.7	6.2	3.7	17.3	333
Ashanti	10.2	29.1	0.8	6.7	4.1	20.8	613
Brong Ahafo	10.7	29.4	1.3	5.7	5.5	20.4	356
Northern	21.8	48.8	1.0	6.6	8.7	35.5	415
Upper East	12.1	31.7	2.4	12.9	7.8	32.4	156
Upper West	12.6	34.1	2.6	11.0	6.0	25.9	95
Total	10.8	29.9	1.3	7.1	4.7	22.1	3,183

37

Note: Each index is expressed in standard deviation units (SD) from the median of
        the NCHS/CDC/WHO International Reference Population.
*Includes children who are below −3 standard deviations (SD) from the International
Reference Population median.
Source: Ghana Statistical Service, Noguchi Memorial Institute for Medical Research
          and ORC Macro. 2004, p.190.

have stunting levels that are above the national average.
With regard to underweight, Volta, Northern, Upper East
and Upper West Regions have above national underweight
levels. It is particularly noted that one in three children in
the Northern Region is underweight.

Prevalence of Anaemia in Children

Table 5 shows the percentage of children aged 6-59
months classified as having anaemia by sex, type of place
of residence and region. The prevalence of anaemia is high
among children in Ghana. Seventy six per cent of children
aged 6-59 months have some level of anaemia including
23% of children who are mildly anaemic, 47% who are
moderately anaemic and 5.8% who are severely anaemic.
The prevalence of anaemia in children is high in rural
areas (80.1%) than in urban areas (67.8%). The highest
prevalence of anaemia among children is found in the
Northern Region (82.5%), whereas the lowest prevalence is
reported for the Greater Accra Region (61.3%). The
Western, Ashanti, Northern, Upper East and Upper West
Regions have prevalence levels of anaemia that are above
the national average. With regard to the severely anaemic,
Table 5 shows that children from the Western, Ashanti,
Brong Ahafo and Upper East Regions are more disadvantaged than children in the other regions.

Table 5 Percentage of children aged 6-59 months classified as having anaemia by sex, type of place of residence and region, Ghana 2003

Characteristic	Anaemia status				
	Any anaemia	Mild anaemia (10.0-10.9 g/dl)	Moderat anaemia (7.0-9.9 g/dl)	Severe anaemia (below 7.0 g/dl)	Number of children
Sex					
Male	76.2	22.5	47.9	5.8	1,481
Female	75.9	23.5	46.7	5.7	1,511
Type of place of residence					
Urban	67.8	26.1	37.8	4.0	984
Rural	80.1	21.5	51.9	6.7	2,008
Region					
Western	80.4	23.8	47.6	9.0	293
Central	76.8	24.5	46.4	5.9	267
Greater Accra	61.3	24.0	33.2	4.1	324
Volta	72.7	25.3	45.6	1.8	255
Eastern	74.4	24.2	46.5	3.7	292
Ashanti	79.0	23.1	48.5	7.4	553
Brong Ahafo	74.9	22.4	45.9	6.6	333
Northern	82.5	18.7	58.1	5.7	403
Upper East	79.1	22.2	49.4	7.5	186
Upper West	78.3	23.9	52.0	2.5	86
Total	76.1	23.0	47.3	5.8	2,992

Note: g/dl = grams per deciliter
Source: Ghana Statistical Service, Noguchi Memorial Institute for Medical Research and ORC Macro. 2004, p.185.

Prevalence and Treatment of Acute Respiratory Infection

Acute respiratory infection (ARI) is among the leading causes of morbidity and mortality among young children in Ghana. To quantify the prevalence of ARI, mothers were asked whether their children under age five had

Table 6 Percentage of children under five years who were ill with a cough accompanied by short, rapid breathing (symptoms of acute respiratory infection (ARI)), and among children who had symptoms of ARI, the percentage for whom treatment was sought from a health facility or provider by sex, type of place of residence and region, Ghana 2003

Characteristic	Percentage of children with symptoms of AR1	Among children with symptoms of AR1, percentage forwhom treatment was sought from a health provider*	Number of children
Sex			
Male	10.9	43.7	1,686
Female	9.2	44.3	1,654
Type of place of residence			
Urban	8.9	53.0	1,114
Rural	10.6	40.2	2,226
Region			
Western	12.5	(41.4)	332
Central	10.6	(22.7)	280
Greater Accra	8.1	(57.9)	366
Volta	20.0	(29.0)	269
Eastern	10.4	(42.7)	337
Ashanti	8.0	(57.1)	622
Brong Ahafo	10.1	(49.9)	366
Northern	7.0	(39.4)	457
Upper East	9.2	(64.8)	206
Upper West	7.5	(50.8)	104
Total	10.0	44.0	3,340

Note: Figures in brackets are based on 25-49 unweighted cases.
*Excludes pharmacy, shop and traditional practitioner.

been ill with a cough accompanied by short, rapid breathing in the two weeks preceding the survey. Mothers whose children had experienced these symptoms were asked whether they sought advice or treatment from a health provider. It should be mentioned that mothers' perception of illness may be subjective and not validated by a medical examination. Table 6 shows the percentage of children under five years who had cough accompanied by short rapid breathing and those with symptoms of ARI taken to a health facility according to selected characteristics.

Also, from Table 6, 10% of children under five years had symptoms of ARI in the two weeks before the survey. Of these, less than half (44%) were taken to a health facility for treatment. There are small differentials in the prevalence of ARI in terms of sex, type of place of residence and region except that the prevalence level of ARI in the Volta Region is twice that of the national average. The Western Region stands out as the region with the second highest prevalence level of ARI (12.5%).

Prevalence and Treatment of Fever

A major manifestation of malaria and other acute infections in children is fever. Although fever can occur throughout the year, malaria is more prevalent during the rainy season, and as such temporal factors must be considered when interpreting the occurrence of fever as an indicator of prevalence of malaria (Ghana Statistical Service and Macro International Inc., 1999). In the 2003 GDHS, mothers were asked whether their children under five years had a fever in the two weeks preceding the survey.

Table 7 shows that one out of five children under five years had fever in the two weeks preceding the survey. Rural-urban differential in prevalence of fever is minimal. However regional differentials in prevalence of fever are substantial. The proportion of children with fever varies from 15.5% in the Northern Region to 30.5% in the Volta region. Whereas 62.5% of the children who had fever took anti malarial drug, the corresponding percentage was lowest in the Central Region (44%).

Table 7 Percentage of children under five years who were ill with fever during the two weeks preceding the survey, and among children with fever, percentage who took anti-malarial drugs and percentage who took anti-malarial drugs the same/next day after developing fever by sex, type of place of residence and region, Ghana 2003

Characteristic	Percentage of Percentage of Children with fever	Percentage who too anti-malarial drug	Percentage who took anti-malarial drug same/next day	Number of children
Sex				
Male	21.7	62.1	42.8	1,686
Female	20.8	63.5	45.7	1,654
Type of place of residence				
Urban	22.4	65.2	49.4	1,114
Rural	20.7	61.4	41.4	2,226
Region				
Western	23.2	67.3	54.9	332
Central	24.3	44.0	37.2	280
Greater Accra	20.9	65.5	42.9	366
Volta	30.5	67.1	50.0	269
Eastern	19.8	66.8	49.8	337
Ashanti	20.4	58.7	42.1	622
Brong Ahafo	18.3	67.0	55.0	366
Northern	15.5	61.0	35.6	457
Upper East	21.3	70.5	31.8	206
Upper West	30.1	66.5	31.3	104
Total	21.3	62.8	44.2	3,340

The prompt treatment of fever by the use of anti-malarial drugs is crucial for infants and children who have fever. Table 7 also shows that prompt treatment of fever was taken by 44% of children who were ill with fever. Children in the Central, Northern, Upper East and Upper West Regions are less likely than other children to receive prompt treatment of fever. More than half of the children in the Western and Brong Ahafo Regions who had fever received prompt treatment of fever.

Prevalence and Treatment of Diarrhoea

The 2003 GDHS asked mothers whether their children under two years had suffered from diarrhoea at any time during the two weeks prior to the survey. If a child had diarrhoea the mother was asked about feeding practices during the diarrhoea episode and about what actions were taken to treat the diarrhoea. Because the prevalence of diarrhoea varies seasonally, the results should be interpreted with caution.

Table 8 presents information on percentage of children under five years with diarrhoea in the two weeks preceding the survey. It is seen that 15.2% of children under five years had diarrhoea in the two weeks prior to the survey. Male children are slightly more likely than female children to have had diarrhoea, whereas rural children are more predisposed to diarrhoea than urban children. There are regional differentials in the prevalence of diarrhoea. The prevalence of diarrhoea ranges from 12.8% in the Greater Accra Region to 26.9% in the Upper West Region.

The percentage of children for whom treatment for diarrhoea was sought from a health facility or provider is surprisingly low; one out of every four children. Male children and children in the urban areas and Upper East Region are more likely to be taken to a health provider for treatment. The pattern of differentials for receipt of oral rehydration therapy (ORT) is the same as that for treatment-seeking for diarrhoea.

Table 8 Percentage of children under five years with diarrhoea in the two weeks preceding the survey, and among children with diarrhoea, the percentage for whom treatment was sought from a health facility or provider, the percentage who received oral rehydration therapy (ORT), by sex, type of place of residence and region, Ghana 2003

Characteristic	Percentage of children with diarrhoea	Percentage taken to a health provider*	ORS packets	Number of children
Sex				
Male	15.9	27.4	41.4	1,686
Female	14.6	23.4	35.5	1,654
Type of place of residence				
Urban	13.6	35.5	47.1	1,114
Rural	16.1	21.3	35.0	2,226
Region				
Western	14.4	(27.2)	(37.0)	332
Central	15.9	(23.8)	(45.2)	280
Greater Accra	12.8	(15.5)	(28.7)	366
Volta	13.3	(9.8)	(36.5)	269
Eastern	15.7	(17.0)	(32.6)	337
Ashanti	14.3	26.7	41.3	622
Brong Ahafo	13.9	28.5	43.5	366
Northern	15.3	29.0	32.4	457
Upper East	20.8	43.0	58.4	206
Upper West	26.9	32.8	29.7	104
Total	15.2	25.5	38.6	3,340

Note: Figures in parentheses are based on 25-49 unweighted cases.
*Excludes pharmacy, shop and traditional practitioner.

Micronutrient Intake Among Children

Micronutrients are essential for the metabolic processes in the body. The 2003 GDHS collected various types of

Table 9 Percentage of youngest children under three years living with the mother who consumed fruits and vegetables rich in vitamin A in the seven days preceding the survey and percentage of children aged 6-59 months who received vitamin A supplements in the six months preceding the survey by sex, type of place of residence and region, Ghana 2003

Characteristic	Consumed fruits and vegetables rich in vitamin A*	Number of children under age three	Consumed vitamin A supplements	Number of children age 6-59 months
Sex				
Male	42.1	934	79.8	1,515
Female	40.3	912	76.9	1,511
Type of place of residence				
Urban	40.8	629	80.6	1,017
Rural	41.5	1,217	77.2	2,009
Region				
Western	40.5	168	80.1	297
Central	49.6	156	66.8	259
Greater Accra	34.5	194	74.3	339
Volta	39.8	151	82.2	242
Eastern	50.5	184	78.4	313
Ashanti	51.3	345	82.0	563
Brong Ahafo	47.7	206	75.1	328
Northern	27.2	263	78.3	409
Upper East	23.9	120	85.5	186
Upper West	34.1	60	84.8	91
Total	41.2	1,846	78.4	3,026

*Includes pumpkin, red or yellow yams or squash, carrots, red sweet potatoes, green leafy vegetables, mango, pawpaw, and other fruits and vegetables that are rich in vitamin A.

data that are useful in assessing the micronutrient status of young children. The information on vitamin A supplements is based on mother's recall and hence results should be interpreted with caution. Table 9 shows the percentage of children under three years who consumed fruits and vegetables rich in vitamin A in the seven days preceding the survey and the percentage of children aged 6-59 months who received vitamin A supplements in the six months preceding the survey.

It is noted in Table 9 that 41% of children under three years who live with their mothers consume fruits and vegetables rich in vitamin A. The Ashanti Region registered the highest percentage (51.3%), while the percent for the Upper East Region is 23.9. More than three out of five children aged 6-59 months are reported to have received vitamin A supplements. There are marked regional differentials in micronutrient intake among children. Consumption of vitamin A supplements is highest in the Upper West Region (84.4%) and lowest in the Central Region (66.8%).

Predictors of receiving Medical Treatment for Diarrhoea

Two logistic regression models are run with (i) receipt of medical treatment for diarrhoea and (ii) receipt of medical treatment for fever/cough as dependent variables. Seven independent variables namely; mother's region of residence, birth order, religion, highest level of education, marital status, type of place of residence and sex of child were entered into the models using the forward stepwise variable selection method. Table 10 presents the results of the logistic regression analysis on receiving medical treatment for episodes of diarrhoea. Of the seven independent variables, mother's region of residence and type of place of residence emerge as the two significant predictors of receipt of medical treatment for diarrhoea. Children born to mothers in the Upper East Region are twice more likely to receive medical treatment for diarrhoea than children whose mothers are from the Northern Region. Part of the advantage of children in the Upper East Region can be explained in terms of treatment-seeking behaviour of their mothers who might have been sensitized through intensive health promotion activities undertaken by the Navrongo Health Research Centre of the Ministry of Health. Children born to urban women are 2.8 times more likely to receive medical treatment for diarrhoea than their rural counterparts.

Table 10 Logistic regression results of receiving medical treatment for diarrhoea by region and type of residence of mothers, Ghana 2003

Characteristic	Logistic coefficient	Odds ratio	P value
Region			
Northern (RC)		1.000	
Western	-0.237	0.789	0.582
Central	-0.220	0.803	0.625
Greater Accra	-1.337	0.263	0.008
Volta	-1.371	0.254	0.029
Eastern	-0.768	0.464	0.095
Ashanti	-0.372	0.689	0.316
Brong Ahafo	-0.307	0.735	0.470
Upper East	0.787	2.196	0.057
Upper West	0.215	1.240	0.661
Type of residence			
Rural (RC)		1.000	
Urban	1.029	2.799	0.000

Constant -1.116
Model X^2 36.802
Df   10
N   580 (unweighted)

Predictors of Receiving Medical Treatment for Fever/Cough

Table 11 shows the results of the logistic regression on receiving medical treatment for fever/cough according to region, type of place of residence and level of education. Once again, children in Upper East have an advantage over children in the other nine regions. Compared with children in the Northern Region (the reference category), they are 2.3 times more likely to receive medical treatment for fever/cough. The type of place of residence has an impact on receipt of medical treatment for

Table 11 Logistic regression results of receiving medical treatment for fever/cough by selected characteristics of mother, Ghana 2003

Characteristic	Logistic coefficient	Odds ratio	P value
Region			
Northern (RC)		1.000	
Western	-0.165	0.848	0.582
Central	-0.569	0.566	0.084
Greater Accra	-0.320	0.661	0.175
Volta	-0.292	0.726	0.287
Eastern	-0.060	0.747	0.348
Ashanti	-0.274	0.942	0.835
Brong Ahafo	-0.307	0.761	0.384
Upper East	0.840	2.316	0.017
Upper West	-0.003	0.997	0.994
Type of residence			
Rural (RC)		1.000	
Urban	0.615	1.850	0.000
Level of education			
No education (RC)		1.000	
Primary	-0.026	0.974	0.888
Secondary	0.441	1.555	0.011

Constant -0.551
Model X^2 51.095
Df   12
N   1104 (unweighted)

fever/cough. Urban children are almost twice more likely to receive medical treatment than rural children. The effect of maternal level of education is also shown in Table 11. Children born to mothers with secondary education are one and a half times more likely to receive medical treatment for fever/cough. Education up to the secondary level can transform a mother's preferences for health care practices so as to significantly improve child health and survival.

Summary and Discussion

This chapter has examined infant and child health inequalities in the 10 regions of Ghana. Infant mortality rate varies from 33 per 1,000 live births in Upper East Region to 105 per 1,000 live births in the Upper West Region. Under-five mortality is also highest in the Upper West Region (208 per 1,000 live births). The attainment of the MDG of reducing under-five mortality by two thirds between 1990 and 2015 is therefore a tall order for the Upper West Region. Central and Volta Regions registered the highest proportions of children 12-23 months who had been fully vaccinated, while the smallest proportion is recorded for the Northern Region. Differentials in any breastfeeding are minimal according to sex and region.

The three anthropometric indices of nutritional status show that 30% of children under-five years are stunted, 7% are wasted, while 22% are underweight. Greater Accra Region has the least proportion of stunted children (13.9%), while 48.8% of children in the Northern Region are stunted. Male children are more likely to be stunted than their female counterparts.

The logistic regression models for receiving medical treatment for diarrhoea and fever/cough indicate the advantage urban children have over rural children. For instance, urban children are 2.8 times more likely to receive medical treatment for diarrhoea than rural children. This advantage is due in part to the lop-sided distribution of social and health care facilities in favour of urban areas to the detriment of the rural areas.

Most of the indicators used to describe infant and child health inequalities show that the Northern Region is the most disadvantaged region, while the Upper East Region stands tall among the three northern regions. Northern Region's disadvantage is partly explained in terms of inadequate number of health institutions which have to serve a large population living in a wide range of dispersed settlements. In 2000, Northern Region had 9.6% of the total population of Ghana but its share of health institutions was 5.7%. In 2000, population per health institution was 14,980 in the Northern Region, 5,682 in the Upper West and 9,456 in the Upper East Region compared with a national average of 8,512 (Ministry of Health, 2001). On the other hand, Upper East's advantage is due in part to its compact nature, availability of child health services and probably the health seeking behaviour of the women which has been somewhat influenced by the health promotion activities of the Navrongo Health Research Centre. Information on availability of child health services shows that the percentage of facilities offering all basic child health services (growth monitoring for healthy children, any routine vaccinations for children at the facility and curative care for children) was 95 for the Upper East Region compared to 78 for the Northern Region (Ghana Statistical Service et al., 2003).

Because of the dispersed nature of localities in the Northern Region, there is the need for the establishment of more health institutions to serve the health needs particularly those of infants and children. The region has to gird its loins so as to be able to catch up with the rest and attain the MDG of reducing under-five mortality by two-thirds by 2015.

References

Ahiadeke, C. 2000. "Breastfeeding, diarrhoea and sanitation as components of infant and child health. A study of large scale survey data from Ghana and Nigeria". *Journal of Biosocial Science*, 32(1):47-61.

Ghana Statistical Service and Macro International Inc. 1999. *Ghana Demographic and Health Survey 1998.* Calverton, Maryland: GSS and MI.

Ghana Statistical Service, Health Research Unit, Ministry of Health and ORC Macro, 2003. *Ghana Service Provision Assessment Survey 2002.* Calverton, Maryland, Ghana Statistical Service and ORC Macro.

Ghana Statistical Service, Noguchi Memorial Institute for Medical Research and ORC Macro, 2004. *Ghana Demographic and Health Survey 2003.* Calverton, Maryland: GSS, NMIMR, and ORC Macro.

Shah, I.H. and J. Khanna, 1990. "Breastfeeding, infant health and child survival in the Asia-Pacific context". *Asia-Pacific Population Journal*, 5(1):25-44.

United Nations, 1994. "Report of the International Conference on Population and Development", Cairo, Egypt, 5-13 September 1994.

Chapter 4

Adolescent Sexuality and Reproductive Health in Ghana: Some Results from a Survey of Cape Coast and Mankrong

Stephen O. Kwankye

Introduction

Adolescent sexuality and reproductive health issues are increasingly becoming of concern in many sub-Saharan African countries. This is especially the case when viewed in the context of the HIV/AIDS pandemic, a situation, which puts many young persons particularly females at risk. This constitutes a serious problem considering that most of these sexual activities are taking place outside wedlock and without contraception. As a result, teenage pregnancies and their accompanying child delinquency and poor development of female adolescent victims are unfolding problems that Ghana will have to contend with for a long time.

One fundamental barrier that has worked seriously against policies that have aimed at addressing adolescent sexuality problems in Ghana has been the socio-cultural environment within which the interventions are being evolved and or implemented. In Ghana, it is felt in many circles that it is culturally unwelcome to discuss sexual issues with adolescents. Again, sections of the society and even some family planning service providers frown upon the provision of family planning services to these youngsters. For example, according to the 1994 Situation Analysis of Family Planning Service Delivery Points in Ghana, 40% of service providers expressed their unwillingness to provide family planning services such as intra-uterine device (IUD) and injectables to unmarried adolescents and 25% of them would not administer the pill under the same conditions (Ghana Statistical Service, 1994).

Such an unfriendly socio-cultural environment has often overtly or covertly not permitted open and frank discussions regarding issues of sexuality and reproductive health particularly among adolescents. Thus, as a result of their engagement in unprotected sex, the chances of further enhancement of their socio-economic development are often and largely foreclosed due to unplanned pregnancies and, or sexually transmitted infections (STIs) including HIV/AIDS. In Ghana, the three Demographic and Health Survey reports of 1993, 1998 and 2003 have indicated that overall a little more than one in every 10 female adolescents of 15-19 years have begun childbearing at a time they are expected to be in school (GSS and MI, 1994; 1999; 2004).

The conditions are again made fertile for criminal abortion to thrive in Ghana. Data are not readily available on abortion in Ghana, but in a society where adolescents are largely indulging in sex with little or no family planning practices, the probability exists for pregnant adolescents who still want to continue their education to resort to induced, and unsafe abortion which is likely to contribute to high maternal mortality ratios in Ghana.

Data on reported AIDS cases in Ghana suggest that a higher proportion of HIV contraction takes place during adolescent ages of 15-19 years. For example, available data on reported AIDS cases by age indicate that for both males and females, almost 75% of the cases were reported among persons aged 20-39 years and 4% among adolescents aged 15-19 years. The inference is that considering that the incubation period of the disease ranges between 5 and 12 years or more, it is possible that many of the reported cases in the age group 20-39 must have been contracted within adolescent ages.

Adolescent childbearing rates in Ghana have been found to be highest in the Central Region in 1993 (33.3%) and 2003 (34.1%) (see GDHS reports of 1993 and 2003). At the same time, the region has been shown to have one of the highest levels of poverty in the country in 1998/1999 (Government of Ghana/UNFPA, 2004).

Linked to the high sexual activity among young women is their low contraceptive use. For example, current contraceptive use for modern methods in 1993 was 5.0% and 8.3% among women of 15-19 and 20-24 years respectively compared to 9.3% among all women in Ghana (Ghana Statistical Service, 1994). The corresponding figures for 1998 were 4.8% and 10.4% among women of 15-19 and 20-24 years respectively as against 10.7% among all women in Ghana. In 2003, modern contraceptive use was 6.4% and 15.4% among married females of 15-19 and 20-24 years respectively compared to 20.7% among all women in the country. The implication is that low contraceptive use among adolescent and young women may foreclose education and employment opportunities to many of them as they expose themselves to risks of unplanned pregnancies.

In addition, social and health problems that arise from early motherhood for both mother and child are not in the interest of the nation's manpower development. For example, teenage pregnancies are contributing to school dropouts, a phenomenon which is impeding the nation's efforts at empowering women through increasing female education.

In view of the foregoing social, health and economic problems that are the result of adolescent sexual behaviour, the relevant questions that this chapter seeks to answer include the following: At what age does sexual activity begin among female adolescents in Cape Coast and Mankrong? What peculiar factors are contributory to the adolescents' decision to enter into sexual activity? To what extent do sexually active female adolescents vary from their sexual partners? To what extent are marriages among female adolescents pregnancy-induced? What are the reproductive health implications of female adolescent sexuality in the context of Ghana's drive towards women empowerment and overall human capital development? and To what extent is Ghana likely to attain the millennium development goal of reducing maternal mortality ration by three-quarters by 2015?

Against the foregoing background and enumerated problems, the chapter has the overall objective of analyzing adolescent sexuality vis-à-vis marriage for the purpose of examining the possible reproductive health implications for female adolescents in Ghana. The specific objectives are to investigate the age at which female adolescents in Cape Coast and Mankrong initiate sexual activity; to examine the factors that affect female adolescents' initiation into sex; to analyse the variations between female adolescents and the sexual partners; to examine the extent to which marriages among female adolescents are pregnancy-induced and; to analyse the reproductive health implications of adolescent sexuality for human capital development not only for the two communities but Ghana as a whole.

Some hypotheses are examined, namely there is an inverse relationship between age at first sexual intercourse and childbearing among female adolescents; and education relates inversely with childbearing among adolescent females. It is further hypothesized that there is an inverse relationship between adolescent childbearing and contraceptive use at first sex.

Sources of Data and Methodology

The analysis is based on primary data collected in a 1997 survey undertaken in Cape Coast, the Central regional capital, and Mankrong, a rural settlement in the region. The two study areas were chosen purposely to facilitate a comparison of adolescent sexual and reproductive health situation in an urban vis-à-vis a rural area.

The total sample was made up of 1,828 females of 12-24 years: 1.503 (82.2%) from Cape Coast and 325 (17.8%) from Mankrong. The selection of the sample in Cape Coast was carried out in two stages. First, Cape Coast was divided into 34 clusters made up of 15 low-income, 11 middle-income and 8 high-income residential areas to form the sampling units based on the Town and Country Planning Department's (TCPD) delineated clusters in the town. Simple random sampling was adopted with a consideration of the geographical location of the clusters. Three clusters were each selected from the high and middle-income residential areas and four from the low-income residential areas. Ten residential clusters were therefore selected for enumeration in Cape Coast. Two sets of questionnaire were administered: a household questionnaire and an individual questionnaire. In the case of Mankrong, a complete survey of the village was undertaken. In both Cape Coast and Mankrong, the individual survey was targeted at adolescent females aged 12-24 years. The analysis also relies on qualitative data collected from focus group discussions (FDGs) separately among female and male young persons of 12-24 years and adult males and females. The qualitative data thus, provided additional information to strengthen the results of the quantitative analysis.

Simple techniques of analysis, including cross tabulations, rates, ratios and proportions are employed. Rigorous statistical analysis could not be attempted due to the small proportion of the sample that had ever had sex, married and or become pregnant. A multiple regression analysis was however, done to attempt a statistical explanation of the relationships between age at first sexual activity and childbearing among adolescents. The validity of the hypotheses was determined at 95% level of confidence. The analysis is limited by the fact that due to the small sample size, the multivariate analysis could not be done separately for each of the two study areas.

Results

Adolescent Sexuality

The reproductive health status of female adolescents anywhere in the world may be assessed and understood first and foremost on the basis of how early in age they start practising sexual intercourse and circumstances within which sexual activity takes place. Against this background, female adolescents in Cape Coast and Mankrong are examined as to what proportion of the sample interviewed had ever had a sexual intercourse and the environment or conditions within which their first sexual activity may be understood.

Age at First Sex

The survey asked the adolescents whether or not they had ever had a sexual intercourse. Table 1 shows that overall, the percentage of adolescents who have ever had sex increases with age. Comparing age groups less than 15, 15-19 and 20-24 years there is a relatively higher percentage of adolescents who had ever had sex in Mankrong, a rural area than in Cape Coast, an urban area. For the entire sample, 37% of the adolescents had ever had a sexual intercourse. Thus, 63% of them had not initiated sex at the time of the survey. Specifically, among adolescents of 15-19 years, 69% were yet to initiate sexual activities. This compares with 62% and 61% respectively from the 1998 and 2003 GDHS reports. Comparing the two study areas however, it is clear that the proportion that ever had sexual intercourse in Mankrong was higher than Cape Coast by almost 10%.

One other significant deduction that could be made from the analysis is that by the age of 20 years, 70.3% (i.e., 121 of 172 adolescents) of the adolescents had ever had sex for the entire sample (figures not shown) compared to more than 85.0% in 1993, 81.4% in 1998 and 70.5% in 2003 as reported in the GDHS studies. For the current study areas, the results indicate that 79.1% of adolescents aged 20 years in Mankrong and 67.4% in Cape Coast had ever had sex at the time of the survey (figures not shown). These figures suggest some improvement on the recorded figures from the 1993, 1998 and 2003 GDHS reports.

Table 1. Percentage Distribution of Adolescents Who Have Ever Had Sex by Current Age in Cape Coast and Mankrong

Current	Cape Coast		Mankrong		Total	
Age	N	%	N	%	N	%
<15	6	6.0	0	0.0	6	1.2
15-19	203	29.5	44	40.0	247	31.0
20-24	327	76.6	99	86.1	426	78.6
Total	536	35.7	143	44.0	679	37.1

Source: Computed from Adolescent Survey, Cape Coast and Mankrong, Aug.-Sept., 1997.

Analysis of the timing of first sexual activity among the adolescents using mean age at first sexual intercourse shows the peak period of first sexual activity to be within 15-19 years while as high as 82% of the adolescents indicated having ever had sexual intercourse (Figure 1). While this is true for both study areas, it is higher in Mankrong (91%) as against Cape Coast (80.0%). Conversely, a relatively higher proportion of the adolescents in Cape Coast had their first sexual experience earlier (i.e. less than 15 years) than their counterparts in Mankrong: almost 10% had sexual intercourse at ages less than 15 years in Cape Coast compared to 4% in Mankrong. There is also a higher proportion of adolescents in Cape Coast initiating sexual intercourse at ages between 20 and 24 years (10%) than in Mankrong (a little less than 5%). This suggests that although a relatively higher proportion of adolescents start sexual intercourse earlier in Cape Coast than at Mankrong, at later ages (20-24 years) one is likely to find a relatively higher proportion of them yet to be initiated into sex in Cape Coast compared to their counterparts in Mankrong.

The foregoing finding may be due to the fact that in the rural areas, adolescents who attain age 20 years without continuing their education, are likely to enter into sexual activity during their teen ages. Thus, during 20-24 years, a relatively fewer proportion of adolescents in rural areas may be left yet to initiate sexual intercourse compared to adolescents in urban areas, most of whom may continue their formal education. One could however, not rule out possible misstatement of age at first sex by adolescents in Mankrong.

Figure 1. Percentage Distribution of Female Adolescents Ever Having Sex by Age at First Sex, Cape Coast and Mankrong

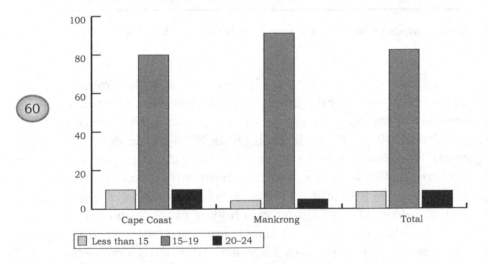

In terms of the mean age at first sexual intercourse, adolescents from the two study areas are almost the same. While in Cape Coast, the mean age at first sexual intercourse was found to be 16.9 years it was 17.0 years in Mankrong. This finding is quite contrary to expectation.

The pattern of distribution of mean age at first sex however, (Table 2) suggests a possible decline in the age at first sexual intercourse for respondents in both study areas. This is because as current age increases, mean age at first sex also generally increases. So far, none of the respondents aged 12-14 years in Mankrong responded to have ever had sexual intercourse. In spite of this, it was found that mean age at first sex for adolescents aged 15-19 years was 16.1 as against 17.4 for those aged 20-24 in Mankrong. Similarly, it was 12.8, 15.9 and 17.5 respectively for respondents aged 12-14, 15-19 and 20-24 years in Cape Coast. It is therefore observed that while the proportion of persons becoming sexually active by the age of 20 years appears to be reducing, the incidence of first sexual intercourse among those who had ever had a sexual experience seems to occur earlier in age than was reported in the 1993 and 1998 GDHS reports (Ghana Statistical Service, 1994 and 1999).

Early age at sex exposes adolescents to reproductive health risks. In Zimbabwe, it has been explained that, "stereotyped sexual norms and peer pressure encourage young males to prove their manhood and enhance their social status by having sex" (Kim et. al., 2001:11). On the other hand, according to Kim et. al., young women are socialized to be submissive and not to discuss sex, thereby leaving them to be unable to refuse sex or insist on condom use.

61

Table 2. Mean Age at First Sex of Adolescents by Current Age, Cape Coast and Mankrong

Current Age	Mean age at first sex - Cape Coast	Mean age at first sex - Mankrong
< 15	12.8	–
15–19	15.9	16.1
20–24	17.5	17.4
Total	16.9	17.0

Source: Computed from Adolescent Survey, Cape Coast and Mankrong, Aug.-Sept., 1997.

Some Factors Affecting the Timing of First Sex

Three factors namely, the living arrangements of adolescents, their level of education and religion have been examined to find out the extent to which they affect the variation of the adolescents in the timing of first sex.

Living Arrangements

The living arrangement is defined broadly as the kind of persons the adolescent is living with in the household. The analysis is premised on the fact that household living conditions and controls may predispose an adolescent to early or later sex due to differences in the care and supervision of adolescents that exist in different kinds of households. Table 3 shows little variation among the adolescents from each study area.

Table 3. Mean Age at First Sex of Adolescents by Living Arrangements, Cape Coast and Mankrong

Living Arrangements	Mean age (years)		Total
	Cape Coast	Mankrong	
Both parents	16.9	16.9	16.9
Father only	17.2	17.4	17.3
Mother only	17.1	17.1	17.1
Other relations	16.5	17.0	16.8
Husband	16.6	16.7	16.7
Friends	17.0	–	17.0
Unrelated person	17.2	17.8	17.5
Alone	18.0*	16.8	17.4

Note: * Represented by one person.
Source: Computed from Adolescent Survey, Cape Coast and Mankrong, Aug.-Sept, 1997.

Level of Education

Analysis of the role of one's education in his/her initiation into sexual intercourse shows a general increasing age at first sexual intercourse with increasing level of education especially in Cape Coast (Table 4). The only inconsistency is with respect to those with primary level education who unexpectedly shows a lower mean age at first sex compared to their counterparts with no education. This could be due to the fact that adolescents with primary education might have dropped out of school as a result of a pregnancy and hence could have a lower age at first sexual intercourse compared to their counterparts with no education.

The foregoing finding appears to be inconsistent with Zabin and Kiragu's (1998) observation that seems to suggest that schooling may actually encourage sexual onset especially as it tends to remove young people from the supervision of traditional caretakers. This explanation may however, lend support to the results of the current analysis of a lower mean age at first sex among adolescents of primary level education relative to others with no education. This could also be the result that adolescents with primary level education might have dropped out of school at the primary level due to a pregnancy. No conclusion could be drawn considering that the stated levels of education relate to the time of the survey and not the timing of the first sexual experience when their level of education might have been different and perhaps lower, a limitation the current study is unable to address.

Table 4. Mean Age at First Sex of Adolescents by Current Level of Education, Cape Coast and Mankrong

Education Level	Mean age (years)	Mean age (years)	Total
	Cape Coast	Mankrong	
No Education	16.0	17.3	16.7
Primary	16.1	17.1	16.4
Arabic	17.0	–	17.0
JSS/Middle	16.8	16.9	16.8
SSS/Secondary	17.1	17.1	17.1
Post-Sec./Higher	18.0	–	18.0
Not stated*	18.0	–	18.0

Note:*Represented by one person.
Source: Computed from Adolescent Survey, Cape Coast and Mankrong, Aug.-Sept., 1997.

Religion

Religion has been found to have a big influence on family life and reproductive health and rights (Familusi, 1999). In the current study however, analysis of the effect of religious differences among the respondents on their mean age at sexual intercourse does not show any marked consistency between the two study areas (Table 5). No significant differences in the mean age at sexual intercourse between the various religious groups were found either. Considering the two study areas, the highest mean age at first sex is recorded among the Muslim group at Mankrong but in Cape Coast, it is among the Catholic and Pentecostal/Charismatic groups followed closely by the Muslim group.

Table 5. Mean Age at First Sex of Adolescents by Religious Affiliation, Cape Coast and Mankrong

Religion	Mean Age at First Sex				Total	
	Cape Coast		Mankrong			
	N	Years	N	Years	N	Years
Catholic	125	17.0	11	16.7	136	17.0
Protestant	196	16.8	53	16.8	249	16.8
Pentecostal/Charismatic	142	17.0	39	17.1	181	17.0
Muslim	55	16.9	25	17.6	80	17.1
Traditional	2	14.5	–	–	2	14.5
No religion	9	16.1	12	17.1	21	16.7
Other	7	15.9	3	15.3	10	15.7
Total	536	16.9	143	17.0	679	16.9

Source: Computed from Adolescent Survey, Cape Coast and Mankrong, Aug.-Sept., 1997.

Characteristics of Sexual Partners of Adolescents

The characteristics of the sexual partners of the adolescents are examined on the premise that sexual activity always takes place between two persons. From Figure 2, it is shown that a higher proportion of adolescents in Mankrong (31.4%) reported having sexual partners compared to Cape Coast (25.9%). With respect to age, more than two-thirds of the male sexual partners are reported by their female partners to be within 20-29 years. About 16% of them are 30 years and over while just about 10% were less than 20 years. Although not much variation is found between the two study areas, a slightly higher proportion of the male sexual partners in the rural area are older (21.6% of them aged 30 years and over) relative to their counterparts in the urban area (15.1%). Correspondingly, a slightly smaller proportion of the male partners in the rural area are aged less than 20 years compared to that of the urban. What is clear is that most of the male sexual partners in both Cape Coast and Mankrong are not of the same ages as their female counterparts.

Figure 2. Percentage Distribution of Sexual Partners of Female Adolescents by Age, Cape Coast and Mankrong

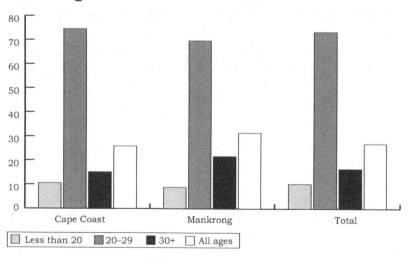

The chapter also examines the variation in age between the females and their male sexual partners at the time of the first sexual encounter of the female adolescent who was interviewed in the survey. In the survey, the female respondents were asked about how old they were at the time of their first sexual encounter as well as the age of the persons with whom they had their first sexual activity.

The comparison between the males and females (Table 6) shows that on the whole, the females are younger than their male partners at their first sexual activity. This suggests that the females have first sex earlier than the males. Agyei and Epema (1990) have documented a similar finding in Kampala, Uganda where mean age at first sexual intercourse was recorded as 15.7 years for adolescent males and 15.3 years for adolescent females. This is however, contrary to Nabila and Fayorsey's (1996) finding in their study of Accra and Kumasi, Ghana with mean age at first sexual intercourse recorded as 15.8 years among the adolescent males and 16.2 years among the females. For almost all the ages reported for first sexual activity to have taken place, the variation clearly depicts the males to be older.

Table 6. Mean Age of Sexual Partner by Age of Adolescent at First Sex, Cape Coast, Mankrong

| Age at | Mean Age of Sexual Partner | | Variation (Years) | |
First Sex	Cape Coast	Mankrong	Cape Coast	Mankrong
8	16.0	–	8.0	–
11	12.0	–	1.0	–
12	14.5	16.5	2.5	4.5
13	17.9	15.0	4.9	2.0
14	19.1	17.3	5.1	3.3
15	19.4	19.6	4.4	4.6
16	21.1	22.1	5.1	6.1
17	21.2	20.7	4.2	3.7
18	23.2	22.0	5.2	4.0
19	23.0	21.4	4.0	2.4
20	23.7	27.7	3.7	7.7
21	20.7	27.0	–0.3	6.0
22	26.6	–	4.6	–
23	25.7	–	2.7	–

Source: Computed from Adolescent Survey, Cape Coast and Mankrong, Aug.-Sept., 1997.

With respect to the type of occupation these sexual partners are engaged in, 1.8% and 26.3% of the total number of adolescents (with sexual partners) in Cape Coast and Mankrong respectively reported that their sexual partners are unemployed while 21.7% in Cape Coast and 2.1% in Mankrong indicated that their sexual partners are students.

Reasons for Adolescents' Initiation into Sexual Activity

Various reasons are often given in response to the question as to why female adolescents take to sexual relationships. Accordingly, the survey asked the female adolescents from both study areas as to what they considered as their reasons for engaging in their first sexual act.

The responses are presented in Table 7 with a control for age although it has earlier been established that majority of the sexually active adolescents have their first sexual activity when they are 15-19 years (80% in Cape Coast and 90% in Mankrong).

Table 7. Percentage Distribution of Female Adolescents by Reason for First Sexual Encounter and Age at First Sex, Cape Coast and Mankrong

| Reason | Age at First Sex | | | | | |
| | Cape Coast | | | Mankrong | | |
	<15	15-19	20+	<15	15–19	20+
Had the urge	0.0	6.3	9.3	33.3	36.2	71.4
Insistence from boyfriend	7.5	10.5	9.3	0.0	0.0	0.0
Peer pressure	11.3	9.6	13.0	16.7	14.6	28.6
Curiosity	9.5	11.0	5.5	0.0	5.4	0.0
Mutual consent	3.8	4.9	13.0	0.0	0.0	0.0
Seduction	22.7	14.4	5.5	33.3	5.4	0.0
Thought was of age	0.0	3.5	13.0	0.0	0.0	0.0
For fun	5.7	2.7	3.7	16.7	0.0	0.0
Expression of love	7.5	4.9	5.5	0.0	9.2	0.0
Was raped	7.5	0.9	0.0	0.0	3.1	0.0
Financial reasons	11.3	8.2	3.7	0.0	14.6	0.0

Convinced/Promises by partner	5.7	7.2	11.1	0.0	3.1	0.0
Can't tell		7.5	9.1	5.5	0.0	3.8	0.0
Not stated		0.0	6.8	1.9	0.0	4.6	0.0
Total %	9.9	80.0	10.1	4.2	90.0	4.9
N	53	429	54	6	130	7

Source: Computed from Adolescent Survey, Cape Coast and Mankrong, Aug.-Sept., 1997.

Adolescents' Knowledge About Sexuality

One fundamental factor that has been identified to affect female adolescent fertility is their poor knowledge in sexuality and reproductive health in general. Thus, many of the young girls enter into sexual relationships without adequate knowledge about what they are in for. They are therefore limited as to how they can either avoid being pregnant or protecting themselves from contracting an STI including HIV/AIDS.

Against this background, this study looked at the level of knowledge of the female adolescent respondents in sexuality and reproduction. They were first asked as to the source from which they had their knowledge about sexuality.

The sources that were mentioned include parents, siblings, teachers and friends. The analysis shows that friends (i.e., peers) of adolescents are the most regular source of information on sexuality issues among the adolescents in both study areas. While 40% of the adolescents in Cape Coast named friends as their source of sexuality information, almost half of their counterparts in Mankrong gave the same response. In fact, in the case of Mankrong, close to half of the adolescents indicate they do not know the source from which they had knowledge about sexuality. It is also found that teachers are the second major source of knowledge of sexuality issues to female adolescents in Cape Coast. In spite of the fact that parents are the first points of contact for adolescents, they did not constitute a major source of information about sexuality: just 9% of the adolescents from

Cape Coast named parents as their source of knowledge about sexuality and none mentioned them in Mankrong. This suggests the low level of parent-daughter communication on reproductive health as far as the respondents in this study are concerned.

An examination of the views of the female adolescents on first sex and pregnancy also shows that about two-thirds of those in Cape Coast are convinced they could become pregnant at their first sexual intercourse and less than half their counterparts in Mankrong have this awareness. Thus, while just about a quarter of the respondents in Cape Coast think they would not be pregnant at first sexual intercourse, as high as 47% of their friends in Mankrong share a similar opinion. Results of the analysis on first sex resulting in a pregnancy are relatively better compared with the finding of Goddard (1995) in Nigeria which pointed to a high proportion of 60% of persons 12-24 years not aware that pregnancy could result from first sexual intercourse. At the same time, Ajayi et. al. (1991) record that half of adolescents in Kenya did not know that first sexual intercourse could produce a pregnancy.

Table 8. Percentage Distribution of Female Adolescents by Current Age and Knowledge as to Whether a Girl can be Pregnant at First Sexual Intercourse, Cape Coast and Mankrong

	Cape Coast					Mankrong				
Current Age	Yes	No	Don't know	Total N	%	Yes	No	Don't know	Total N	%
<15	43.4	42.7	13.9	479	100.0	17.2	78.8	4.0	99	100.0
15-19	69.7	23.3	7.0	687	100.0	55.4	38.2	6.4	110	100.0
20-24	86.9	10.3	2.8	427	100.0	69.0	27.6	3.4	116	100.0
Total N	1,019	370	114	1,503	100.0	158	152	15	325	100.0
%	67.8	24.6	7.6	–	100.0	48.6	46.6	4.6	–	100.0

Source: Computed from Adolescent Survey, Cape Coast and Mankrong, Aug.-Sept., 1997.

Age at First Marriage

Analysis of the data shows that only a small proportion (5.3% in Cape Coast and 20.0% in Mankrong) of the respondents have ever been married. A higher proportion of the few who have ever been married are also between 20 and 24 years.

Furthermore, the mean age at first marriage increases with age, suggesting that among those who have ever married, there appears to be a declining age at marriage over the years. It is however, noteworthy to state that a large proportion of the respondents especially the young ones were still not married at the time of the survey. The tendency for them to postpone marriage cannot therefore be in doubt.

A comparison of the respondents in the two study areas, on the other hand, shows that those in Mankrong have a relatively lower overall mean age at marriage than their counterparts in Cape Coast. The difference between them is, however, negligible.

Table 9. Mean Age at First Marriage by Current Age of Female Adolescents, Cape Coast and Mankrong

Current Age	Mean age at first marriage		
	Cape Coast	Mankrong	Both
17	17.0*	–	17*
18	18.0*	15.0*	16.5
19	17.9	18.1	18.0
20	18.6	18.4	18.5
21	19.6	18.6	19.0
22	19.7	19.4	19.7
23	19.3	21.2	20.5
24	20.9	21.3	21.0
Total	19.7	19.4	19.5

Note: *Only one person is involved
Source: Computed from Adolescent Survey, Cape Coast and Mankrong, Aug.-Sept. 1997.

Most participants in the focus group discussions felt that the ideal age for a woman to marry is between 20 and 25 years. There were a few who thought it is ideal to marry between 18 and 20 years. No one however, favoured marriage below 18 years, which is quite supportive of the minimum age at marriage in Ghana, which is fixed at 18 years. However, evidence from Table 9 shows some inconsistency with views gathered from the focus group discussions. This is because although during the discussions, both adults and adolescents were all unanimously not in favour of any marriage below 18 years, there were some adolescents who had already been married below 18 years. What one considers as ideal is therefore, quite different from what occurs in practice.

One observation from the analysis is that at all ages at marriage, the males are older than their female partners (figures not shown). A similar observation is made comparing age at first marriage within ages less than 20 years and 20-24 years, the marriage partners of female adolescents in Mankrong having relatively higher ages than their counterparts from Cape Coast. This is quite normal since in Ghana there is always a higher tendency for males to marry women who are younger than they are.

It is found that the male partners in Mankrong are on the average one year older than their male counterparts in Cape Coast. This is supported by the observation that with the exception of women who married at age 22 years, the variation in age is higher for males in Mankrong than those in Cape Coast at all the ages at first marriage (figures not shown). The variation found here is consistent with the earlier observation when the ages of the females and those of their male partners at the time of first sexual intercourse were examined. This however, does not loose sight of possible misstatement of ages of male sexual partners by adolescent females who were interviewed in the survey.

Decision to Marry

The decision to marry is examined to find out to what extent marriages among female adolescents are pregnancy-induced. In other words, do they marry because of a pregnancy at a time they were not married? It is observed that many adolescent marriages are the result of unexpected pregnancies. It therefore means that many of them might not have married at the time they did but for the pregnancy they had. There is, however, a variation between respondents in Cape Coast and Mankrong. Overall, more than half of the young females ever marrying in Mankrong said their first marriages were pregnancy-induced compared to 43% of those in Cape Coast (Table 10). It should however be noted that for a majority of the adolescents who have ever married, their decision to marry is influenced by their sexual partners apart from their own personal decision to marry at the time they do (figures not shown).

Table 10. Percentage of Female Adolescents in Respect of Whether their Marriages were Pregnancy-Induced by Age at First Marriage, Cape Coast and Mankrong

Age at	Cape Coast				Mankrong			
Marriage	Pregnancy induced		Not pregnancy induced		Pregnancy induced		Not pregnancy induced	
	N	%	N	%	N	%	N	%
<20	13	39.4	20	60.6	24	68.6	11	31.4
20-24	21	42.0	29	58.0	12	40.0	18	60.0
Total	34	42.5	49	57.5	36	55.4	29	44.6

Source: Computed from Adolescent Survey, Cape Coast and Mankrong, Aug.-Sept., 1997.

The proportion of the marriages said to be pregnancy-induced is found to be quite substantial particularly for Mankrong. It is therefore not surprising that Ajayi et. al. (1991) report in their study in Kenya that age at birth of first child tends to parallel age at first marriage. It is also noteworthy to state that comparing marriages at less than 20 years to those at 20-24 years, the proportion of the marriages reported to be pregnancy-induced in Cape Coast was relatively higher among marriages at 20-24 years (42.0%) than at less than 20 years (39.4%). This is however, in sharp contrast with the situation in Mankrong where the figures are 68.6% among marriages at less than 20 years and 40.0% among those taking place between 20 and 24 years. The foregoing observation suggests that if unwanted or unplanned pregnancies and first births among the adolescents could be avoided, marriages could be delayed or postponed till later ages when it would be physiologically more ideal and healthy to participate in childbearing. The analysis, however, does not lose sight of the small number of respondents that are involved, which could introduce some biases.

The conclusion that may be drawn from this analysis is that majority of the female adolescents are not in favour of early marriages. Yet, it appears that many of them learn mainly by experiencing the events before advising themselves to the contrary. It is obvious that to forestall this practice, young adolescents should not be denied reproductive health education from both parents and teachers. Again, the views of parents regarding whom to marry should not be imposed on the adolescents. Instead, adolescents should be guided to make the right decisions. This is consistent with the views expressed by both adults and adolescents in the focus group discussions.

The Relationship between Sexuality and Childbearing

The analysis using multiple regression examined the relationship between number of pregnancies ever had by adolescents as the dependent variable and a number of independent variables including current age of the respondent, her educational level, age at first sex, marital status, knowledge of contraception, the ovulatory cycle and contraceptive use at first sex. From the results shown in Table 11, age appears to relate positively with number of pregnancies ever had by the adolescent females. This is to be expected since older adolescents are likely to have a longer period of sexual exposure relative to their younger counterparts. Besides, a relatively higher proportion of the youth of 20-24 years were found to have ever been married. Thus, since marriage exposes women to a higher risk of pregnancy, it follows as a matter of course that pregnancy incidence will increase with higher age of the woman especially in a society where contraceptive use particularly among adolescents is quite low. Overall, the variables included in the model explained 40% of the variation in the number of pregnancies ever had.

The results in Table 11 are a confirmation of the hypothesis of an inverse relationship between age at first sexual intercourse and childbearing among adolescents. Thus, increasing age at first sexual intercourse produces declining number of pregnancies among the female adolescents. Specifically, a unit increase in age at first sex results in 0.10 unit reduction in the number of pregnancies ever had (and for that matter childbearing risks) at 100% level of confidence. This supports the observation that substantial delay in first sexual practice among females is likely to contribute largely to higher reduction in unplanned pregnancies.

Besides, the educational level of the adolescent was found to relate inversely with the number of pregnancies she will ever have. In other words, there is the possibility of childbearing relating indirectly with an adolescent's level of education. This finding therefore validates the hypothesis that education relates inversely with childbearing among adolescent females. The results are statistically significant at 100% level of accuracy for almost all levels of education. For example, Post-Secondary/ Higher level of education of the adolescent reduces number of pregnancies ever had by 0.86 compared to adolescents who have no education.

The results further show that contraceptive use at first sex appears to relate indirectly with childbearing risks, i.e., number of pregnancies ever had. Quite clearly, female adolescents who do not practise contraception at their first sexual activity have 0.18 unit increase in number of pregnancies ever had compared to others who practise contraception at first sexual intercourse.

Table 11. Results of Multiple Regression Analysis on Number of Pregnancies Ever Had by Selected Variables in Respect of Adolescent Females in Cape Coast and Mankrong.

Variable	B	S.E	Beta	P value
Age	.1363	.0140	.3723	.0088
Education				
No Education	RC			
Primary	−.2711	.1094	−.1048	.0135
Middle/JSS	−.3998	.0935	−.2198	.0000
Secondary/SSS	−.5369	.1084	−.2500	.0000
Post Secondary/Higher	−.8626	.1474	−.2295	.0000
Contraceptive Use at First Sex				
Yes	RC			
No	.1817	.0646	.0994	.0050
Knowledge of Ovulatory Cycle				
Yes	RC			
No	-.0990	.0586	.0536	.0917
Knowledge of Contraception				
Yes	RC			
No	.2491	.0949	.0959	.0088
Age at First Sex	−.1054	.0164	−.2268	.0000
Marital Status				
Never Married	RC			
Currently Married	.7685	.0772	.3378	.0000
Previously Married	.5858	.2190	.0817	.0077
Constant	−.2492	.2935	−	.3960

R Squared = .4010
Adjusted R = .3912
F = 40.60
Signif. = .0000
R.C. = Reference Category

Adolescent Sexuality and Reproductive Health in Ghana

This is statistically significant at 100% level of confidence, and hence, validates the hypothesis that there is an inverse relationship between adolescent childbearing and contraceptive use at first sex. Similar results are observed in respect of the relationship between contraceptive knowledge and number of pregnancies ever had. Here, at about 99% level of confidence, adolescents who have no knowledge about any method of contraception show a 0.24 unit increase in the number of pregnancies ever had compared to their counterparts who have some knowledge of contraceptive methods.

While these findings point to positive developments, they do suggest that more public education should be done among the general population in Ghana particularly among the adolescents. This is on account of the apparent misconceptions among many adolescent and adult respondents during the focus group discussions as to whether unmarried sexually active adolescent females should use contraception. Incidentally, their views, particularly in Cape Coast, that the exposure of adolescents to contraceptive knowledge and use by the sexually active among them would lead to sexual promiscuity and negative reproductive health impacts on the adolescents are not supported by the regression analysis, the results of which are presented in Table 11.

On the other hand, knowledge of the ovulatory cycle, i.e., when in a woman's reproductive cycle she is likely to be pregnant, does show a contrary relationship with pregnancy incidence. The observation in Table 11 shows that female adolescents who have no knowledge of the ovulatory cycle have 0.10 unit reduction in the number of pregnancies ever had in comparison with their counterparts who indicated knowledge of the ovulatory cycle. This is significant statistically at 90% level of confidence. This is unexpected since ideally, knowledge of when a woman could be pregnant during her reproductive cycle could be an important asset if she wants to avoid an unwanted pregnancy. It is however, possible that girls who have ever become pregnant learnt of when a woman could be pregnant during her ovulatory cycle as a matter of experience. Further research in respect of this relationship would therefore be useful.

Finally, as expected, the analysis shows quite clearly that marriage among adolescents has the tendency to increase number of pregnancies. The evidence is that currently married female adolescents have 0.76 unit increase in number of pregnancies ever had compared to their counterparts who have never married. The increase in respect of adolescents who were previously married is 0.58 in comparison with those who have never married. These results are statistically significant at 100% and 99% level of confidence respectively among currently married and previously married female adolescents (Table 11).

On the whole, the major explanatory factors for the variation in age at first sexual intercourse among the female adolescents in the two study areas (based on the level of significance) have been the adolescents' current age and contraceptive use at first sex. These factors therefore, form the basis for a female adolescent's involvement in first sexual activity. In addition to these factors, contraceptive knowledge, marital status and current level of education were found as the most important factors in understanding the variation in the number of pregnancies ever experienced among the female adolescents.

Discussion

From the analysis, adolescents currently living with their husbands have the lowest mean age at first sexual intercourse, due plausibly to early marriage implying the coincidence of sexual activity and marriage even in situations where the young girl has never had sex before marriage. It is also possible that having indulged in early sex that might have resulted in a pregnancy, marriage becomes a matter of course for most of the young girls. It is plausible that while early marriage could lead to early age at a woman's introduction to sexual intercourse, at the same time, early age at sexual intercourse could result in early marriage.

It became apparently clear that females become sexually active earlier than males contrary to findings recorded by researchers such as Nabila et. al. (1996). However, it could be argued that when males are interviewed about differences in ages between them and their female counterparts, they might appear to have been younger than their female partners at the time of the first sexual act. What perhaps is the situation is that anyone who engages in first sexual activity does so normally with a more sexually experienced partner who is more likely to be older. Therefore, the question as to which of the sexes enters into sexual activity earlier would depend on whether the responses are from males or females. What may bring out a more reliable result would be when males are interviewed separately from the females and their ages at first sex compared instead of resorting to the differences in age between persons who are sexual partners both of whom may not necessarily have their first sexual activity with each other at the same time.

It came out in the focus group discussions that often it is wealthy adults who entice unsuspecting adolescents into sexual relationships. Some of the adults in Mankrong were of the opinion that the discussions should not focus on only perceived wealthy older men taking advantage of young girls but also older rich women who engage young boys for sex, i.e., "sugar daddies" (older men and adolescent girls) and "sugar mammies" (older ladies and adolescent boys). They consequently, condemned this kind of sexual relationship as breeding disrespect between the young and the elderly.

However, one male adult narrated a case where he said he overheard two young females having a chat, alluding to the fact that it is better to have a sexual relationship with an elderly person than with their age mates. According to him, the young women argued that "the young men are not responsible enough and are always ready to deceive and disappoint you while the elderly people will not on account of their experience". It therefore, from his view, appears that it depends on the impression the individual has but it is not a good thing.

The views expressed by most of the adolescents are also interesting. Although they all invariably do not endorse such a relationship, it appears that for financial reasons, they accept it if they are in a position to benefit from the relationship. For example, while some said "it is not good to have someone as old as your father as your sexual partner as it could lead to disrespect", there were others who argued that it could be acceptable because "some of them take good care of the girls". For financial reasons therefore, some of them feel it is good. As one girl remarked, "it is good to have a rich man who will take care of the girl and her boyfriend as well". What this implied was that some of the girls who befriend older men have boyfriends of their age and hence, get funds from the older persons to take care of themselves and their young sexual partners as well. Clearly, this is a recipe for the spread of sexually transmitted infections (STIs) including HIV/AIDS.

The bottom line of all this as further explained by one adolescent female in Mankrong is money. She argued that if the young girl is well catered for at home by her parents or is working and is able to cater for her basic needs, most young girls would not give in to sexual offers by older persons. However, some give in to sexual offers by older persons. Some of them even were of the opinion that some parents do encourage their young girls to go into such sexual relationships with rich but older men because of financial gains they (the parents) hope to benefit from rather than seeking the interest of their daughters.

One striking observation is that the male sexual partners are much older than their female counterparts, suggesting perhaps that the male partners may not be mostly adolescents. This is however, not conclusive since the method of data collection adopted in this study does not in the strict sense permit a comparison between males and females as to which of them on the average is likely to enter into sexual activity earlier. This is especially the case when females who may not know the exact ages of their male counterparts supply the information on the sexual partners. The foregoing suggests that it would be more instructive in future research to have a control group of male adolescents studied alongside the females.

It has been found that sexual activity that take place at ages less than 15 years is mainly the result of seduction by perhaps their unsuspecting much older and more experienced male partners. It suggests that most of the young adolescent females might have responded out of ignorance.

Another important observation has been that peer pressure is a relatively strong driving force behind many female adolescents' entry into first sex. For example, it has been reported that as part of peer pressure, some girls may have no choice but to submit to the sexual demands of boyfriends who threaten to abandon them if they refuse to comply with the boys' sexual advances (Goldstein, 1993; Preston-Whyte, 1994). As has been noted earlier, peer pressure and financial reasons are the second major reasons cited among the adolescents who had their first sexual intercourse under 15 years in Cape Coast and the third in Mankrong. This means, they only follow their peers without much independent assessment of the costs and benefits of sexual intercourse at these early ages. There is therefore the need for education on sexual issues at early ages both at the household and school levels to avoid these peer pressures, much of which could be quite negative to the future development of the adolescents.

Furthermore, a considerable proportion of the adolescents suggested their first sexual activity was due to financial reasons, an observation which is consistent with Nabila and Fayorsey's (1996) finding that many adolescents in Accra and Kumasi indulge in sexual activity due to poverty-related circumstances. In reality, poverty among parents could pre-dispose their adolescent children to have sex in order to earn some money to support themselves. In a similar vein, Olawoye (1995) reports that adolescents point to overcrowding living conditions that allow children to observe parental sexual intimacy and to the prevalence of rape. This, to a large extent, is the result of poverty making adolescents take to sex for financial reasons. A small number of them (less than 10%), however, indicated that their first sexual encounter was actually an expression of love. Unfortunately, some of them (7.5% of adolescents in Cape Coast whose first sex occurred at ages less than 15 years for example) said they were raped which puts such female adolescents at risk of becoming pregnant or contracting sexually transmitted infections including HIV/AIDS since rapists usually do not have protected sex with their victims. It also suggests that many rape cases take place in Ghana than is reported.

Majority of the adolescents studied do not support pre-marital sex, based mainly on religious prohibitions. About 54% of female adolescents in Cape Coast support this reason while the figure for Mankrong is 41%. Ironically, however, it appears that many adolescents who quote these reasons to support their views on pre-marital sex do not heed these religious inhibitions against pre-marital sex, otherwise we would find a much lower percentage of female adolescents ever having sexual intercourse than it is otherwise recorded.

In the focus group discussions, most of the discussants, adults and adolescents, thought it is not good for unmarried persons to have sexual relationships. Various reasons were given in support of this opinion. A few of them, however, thought otherwise, with apparent reference to the circumstances many adolescents find themselves in most cases.

One female adult in Cape Coast was emphatic that most of the unmarried adolescents are actually dragged into sexual activity by adults. In other words, many adolescents would stay without practising sex until marriage but for the role of older persons. In her own words, "the elderly men are responsible for the current sexual activity of most of the adolescents. In cases where adolescents refuse such sexual advances of adult men, they are accused of being disrespectful".

The others explained the situation within the context of so-called modernisation of the Ghanaian society, which has glorified sexual relationships involving unmarried adolescents as a modern practice. According to them, this is a marked departure from what prevailed several years ago when it was societally abominable for sexual relationships to precede marriage.

On the part of many of the adolescents in Cape Coast, sex before marriage is generally not considered good but acceptable if that is the only means by which they could survive. Here, it is a question of monetary gains. According to one of them, this usually happens when parents are unable to provide for the needs of their children. In this case, if under such a situation a gentleman will have sex with a female and provide the money to support her, she does not see anything wrong with it since it is a matter of one's survival. In her own words, "there are young girls who desire to have some money to trade but their parents refuse to give it to them. At the same time, even when they see their friends with new clothes, they also yearn for such items. In the circumstance, if they find a man who is willing to provide these items, they yield to their sexual advances".

One adolescent on the other hand, linked it to peer pressure. To her, when they see their friends practising sex, they consider it to be fashionable and so they join. There were, however, some adolescents who condemned it out-rightly on account of the hardships it may bring to innocent children who may be born through such pre-marital sexual relationships. On the contrary, one adolescent was convinced that "pre-marital sex is good and acceptable since that is the only way one could prepare and get the experience about marriage before entering the marriage institution itself".

From the foregoing, it could be concluded that majority of the respondents in the focus group discussions, whether adults or adolescents, do not seem to agree that adolescents should have pre-marital sex. Yet, it is clear from the analysis that pre-marital sex has become quite unavoidable among some adolescents in Ghana. It therefore appears that given the option, many adolescents will choose abstinence but are unable to do that for financial reasons as well as pressure from their peers as some of the adolescents openly expressed. Since the inability of parents to provide for the needs of their female adolescents is cited as a major reason, the role of parents in the attainment of this goal of sexual abstinence before marriage becomes quite critical.

On the factors that were thought by the adolescents in the focus group discussions to contribute to their early entry into sexual unions, most of the responses in either study area are mixed in the sense that while some of them blame the development on the inability of most parents to either meet the needs of their children or instil discipline and moral values in them, others think it is due to the inability of some adolescents to abide by parental guidance. They all invariably agree that sexual activity involving adolescents is quite early. In support of this claim, one adult male for example, indicated that "it is being done openly at Victoria Park in Cape Coast" and hence there is no secret about it.

In either Cape Coast or Mankrong, there is some consensus among the adults that many parents are going through economic hardships and hence, are unable to discharge their financial obligations to their children. For example, some parents have no jobs and cannot cater for their wards. Another dimension of the problem is also explained in terms of the absence of one or both parents from home most often in search of money to keep the household running. They are therefore not always at home to keep an eye on their children in order to provide the needed guidance. However, they thought that the demands of some adolescents are insatiable considering the poor financial status of most of their parents. The inability of parents to satisfy the many material desires of their children therefore often draws them into relationships that may end up in sex at early ages in life.

The issue of broken homes was also cited as a major contributory factor during the focus group discussions.

Many of the adults explained for example that, in broken homes, most often, neither the father nor mother is in control. In the process, some children are left to care for themselves leaving them with no option than to enter into sexual relationships for financial gains. According to some of them, the situation is made worse when the children have to live with their mothers as single parents, who, most often do not have much control over the children. Some of the adolescents made similar arguments. On the other hand, misunderstanding between parents especially when they are not in agreement regarding how their children should be disciplined, could pre-dispose the children to practise sexual activity at early ages. For example, one male adult explained that, "some mothers stand behind their daughters any time their fathers discipline them about their sexual habits. Some mothers could even team up with their daughters against the father who, may be considered as being harsh and in the process, push the poor daughter into sexual relationships, the consequence of which, she will realise only when it is too late to make amends".

There are still others who attribute early sex to the thinking of some adolescents that their parents are old-fashioned and hence would not take the wise counsel they are provided. Reference was also made to programmes that are shown on the television, which they considered to have both positive and negative influences on the sexual behaviour of adolescents. This is because some of the adolescents are unable to distinguish between the positive and negative things that are screened on the television. As one of them said, most of the films especially the foreign ones are full of sexual episodes which some adolescents try to copy without understanding what they all mean.

Some also blamed early sex among adolescents on some of the cultural practices that are taught in schools, which they felt have sexual underpinnings. The adolescents in Cape Coast in particular made references to the practice of many of their counterparts in imitating certain foreign cultures such as dressing which tends to expose their bodies, making them fall prey to the lustful desires of some unscrupulous men.

The adolescents were to some extent in agreement with their adult counterparts in explaining that both parents and adolescents are to blame. About the role of the parents, they said some of them are not responsible enough as to take care of the needs of their children. Majority of them were however, of the opinion that it is mainly the result of peer pressure that makes some of them follow their friends blindly without actually understanding why they behave the way they do. In the words of one adolescent in Mankrong "there is no work here apart from selling coconut. So when a female adolescent finds a friend to be wearing a new dress and realises that she has a boyfriend who sells coconut, she will also be desirous to take a boyfriend who sells coconut in order for her to buy a new dress like her other friend".

In the light of the foregoing, it is quite clear that whether it is parental irresponsibility or peer pressure, the bottom line most often is that of material or financial benefits that will be derived from the sexual relationships. This should be viewed against the background of many of the respondents stating that pre-marital sex is unacceptable.

Knowledge that first sexual intercourse could result in a pregnancy was found to increase with the age of the adolescent with obviously higher knowledge in Cape Coast than Mankrong. In each age group however, particularly in ages less than 20 years, the proportion not knowing that first sexual intercourse could produce a pregnancy, was quite substantial. A much higher proportion of adolescents with no knowledge that first sexual intercourse could result in a pregnancy has however, been found in Kenya where 50% of adolescents did not know that first sexual intercourse could produce a pregnancy (Ajayi et. al., 1991)[11]. The need for more sexuality education at early ages for adolescents can, therefore, not be over-emphasised. This is especially an important consideration in view of the fact that the adolescents are limited in the sources of knowledge of sexuality i.e., from their friends (who may not even have the right information) and teachers. Accordingly, quite a substantial proportion of them are not aware that they could be pregnant at their first sexual encounter, a situation that could result in unprotected sexual activity.

The analysis has shown a high knowledge among the adolescents of the possible problems that could result from early sexual practices. This study finds it quite inconsistent that many adolescents would practise sexual activity as if there is nothing at stake. It is therefore clear that in sexual issues among adolescents, knowledge is not the problem but how they could be empowered practically to either fully abstain or practise safer sex, which may involve contraception against either unplanned pregnancy or STI or both.

One fundamental dilemma that needs to be highlighted is the conflict between the policy, legal framework and the socio-cultural environment regarding adolescent sexuality, reproductive health and rights in Ghana. From the International Conference on Population and Development (ICPD), reproductive health is defined as "a state of complete physical, mental and social well-being and not merely the absence of disease or infirmity in all matters related to the reproductive system and its functions and processes". By this definition, it implies people are able to have a satisfying and safe sex life and that they have the capability to reproduce and the freedom to decide if, when, and how often to do so.

However, while the Adolescent Reproductive Health Policy (2000), provides that sexually active adolescents (10-19 years) should have access to reproductive health services including contraceptives, the law on defilement appears to prohibit sexual activity at ages less than 16 years, and by extension, effective denial of this category of adolescents reproductive health services irrespective of their sexual activity status. Such a conflict poses difficulties in reproductive health service delivery to adolescents in Ghana in an environment where socio-culturally, adolescent sexuality issues are shrouded in secrecy and if left unresolved, is likely to pose problems towards the millennium development goal of reducing maternal mortality by three-quarters by the year 2015. This is on account of the fact that maternal mortality tends to be highest among adolescents who begin childbearing at such early ages.

Recommendations

One way to overcome the socio-cultural barrier inhibiting open discussion and counselling of young persons about their sexuality is the establishment of institutions with the expertise on youth counseling. In Ghana, the Planned Parenthood Association of Ghana (PPAG) has established a few youth counselling centres under the "Young and Wise" programme in which the youth themselves are involved as facilitators. With this good beginning by the PPAG, it is recommended that Parliament should consider passing an act that would enjoin each District Assembly in the country to establish at least one District Youth Centre where all young persons in the district could go for recreation and counselling on all issues including sexual and reproductive health. This is considered very important in view of the fact that in Ghana many parents are not equipped to effectively counsel their children on sexual and reproductive health issues. The National Population Council (NPC) and the National Youth Council (NYC) should spearhead this agenda to facilitate the passage and implementation of such a law.

It has been found that many of the adolescents tend to have sex with older persons for financial considerations due to their parents' inability to meet their needs. It is therefore recommended that the campaign on having small family sizes should be intensified throughout the country. Alongside these campaigns, government should find measures to address the issue of low wages and salaries of workers in Ghana so that they (workers) could in turn adequately take care of their children in order that the children would not take sex as an alternative to meet their needs.

In terms of future research, one limitation of this study is its failure to collect information on the education of the adolescents at first sexual intercourse. Thus, it could not analyse very well the effect of education on a person's timing of first sexual activity. Future research should therefore consider collecting information on one's education at the time of first sex to facilitate such an important analysis. Future research should additionally collect information on adolescents' future aspirations pertaining to education as a proxy, which when related to current educational level of the adolescent could offer plausible answers to the relationship between adolescents' education and the timing of their sexual activity.

There is a need for a national comprehensive study that focuses on both male and female adolescents to be able to compare the relevant factors that affect adolescent sexual and reproductive health in the various regions. Such a national research would also have the advantage of understanding the socio-cultural ramifications of the problem from the regional perspectives. This is due to the fact that the demographic and health surveys do not allow in-depth analysis of adolescent sexuality and reproductive health with its restriction of data collection to women 15 years and above.

Finally, there is an urgent need to reconcile the conflicts between the policy environment and the legal framework in the country to ensure smooth sexual and reproductive health information and service delivery to all persons including adolescents of all ages between ages 10 and 19 years.

References

Agyei WK. and Epema E. Adolescent Fertility in Kampala, Uganda: Knowledge,Perceptions and Practice. *Biology and Society.*1990, 7(4): 203-214.

Ajayi, A.A., Marangu, L.T., Miller, J and Paxman, J.M. (1991). Adolescent Sexuality and Fertility in Kenya: a survey of knowledge, perceptions and practices. *Studies in Family Planning,* 1991, July-August: 205-216.

Familusi, A. Gender in Adolescent Reproductive Health – Women to the Fire. *Choices.* 1999, September, 1(3): 16.

Ghana Statistical Service (GSS). A Situation Analysis Study of Family Planning Service Delivery Points in Ghana. 1994, GSS, Accra, Ghana.

Ghana Statistical Service and Macro International Inc. (MI). Ghana Demographic and Health Survey 1993. 1994, Calverton, Maryland.

Ghana Statistical Service and Macro International Inc. (MI). Ghana Demographic and Health Survey 1993. 1998, Calverton, Maryland.

Ghana Statistical Service and Macro International Inc. (MI). Ghana Demographic and Health Survey 2003. 2004, Calverton, Maryland.

Goddard, C. Adolescent Sexuality in Nigeria. The Facts. Advocates for Youth, 1995, Washington, D.C.

Goldstein, D. The Cultural Class and Gender Politics of a Modern Disease: Women and AIDS in Brazil, 1993, Rio de Jereiro and Sao Paulo.

Government of Ghana. Adolescent Reproductive Health Policy. National Population Council. 2000, Accra

Government of Ghana/UNFPA 2004. *State of Ghana Population Report 2003: Population, Poverty and Development.* Government of Ghana/UNFPA, Accra.

Kim, Y..M, Kols, A., Nyakauru, R., Marangwanda, C. and Chibatamato, P. (1997).

Promoting Sexual Responsibility Among Young People in Zimbabwe, *International Family Planning Perspectives*, 2001, 27 (1): 11-18.

Nabila, J.S & Fayorsey, C. (1996). Adolescent Fertility and Reproductive Health Behaviour in Ghana: A Case Study of Accra and Kumasi. *FADEP Technical Series* No. 7, 1996, University of Ghana, Legon.

Olawoye, J. (1995). Adolescent Sexuality in Nigeria: A Research Update. *Network (Nigeria)*. December (2): 11-14.

Preston-Whyte, E. (1994). "Gender and the Lost Generation: The Dynamics of HIV Transmission Among Black South African Teenagers in Kwazulu, Natal". *Health Review*. Supplement to Volume 4: 241-255.

Zabin, L.S. and Kiragu, K. The Health Consequences of Adolescent Sexual and Fertility Behaviour in sub-Saharan Africa. *Studies in Family Planning*, 1998, June, 29(2): 210-232.

Chapter 5

Population Growth, Water/Sanitation and Health

S. K. Gaisie and P. G. Gyau-Boakye

Introduction

Mortality is directly influenced by health. Health services are utilized to reduce mortality and to prolong life. Clean water and sanitation also have a considerable effect on reducing mortality and morbidity. In fact, water is a necessary condition for human existence. Life is therefore sustained by continuous circulation of water. Improved health depends on increasing household water supplies.

Population expansion tends to engender severe water sustainability problems such as rapidly increasing water scarcity (and/or food scarcity) and protection of water quality in order to avoid the menace of water-related diseases (e.g. diarrhoea, cholera, guinea worm etc.). It has been estimated that, in addition to rising demand, continued population growth implies that the actual ceiling of the affordable water use would decrease to half its present level when the population doubles its size and to a quarter when it quadruples its size (Falknermark, 1990). Population growth therefore consumes potentially available water in order to meet an increasing water demand. The influence on population of natural resource constraints is reflected, among other things, in water scarcity that generates high levels of morbidity among the population.

Development involves, among other things, meeting rising water demand for improved health, quality of life, and food security. Population expansion, as noted earlier on, places severe constraints on the water availability to achieve these goals. Thus, as a result of water shortages, it is increasingly becoming an uphill task to provide for future improvements in the quality of life. Consequently, increasing water scarcity in response to unavoidable population growth and food and water needs that go with it forms the greatest challenge for humanity to address.

There is therefore the need to raise awareness of increasing water shortage due to rapid population expansion so that realistic policy options to reduce the threat can be identified and urgently formulated and implemented. This is crucial for the ongoing poverty reduction programme because poverty reduction in a developing country is critical for sustainable development.

This chapter attempts to assess the amount of water available for use in the Volta, South Western and Coastal river systems; estimate the percentage of the overall availability that can be made accessible for withdrawal; determine the relationship between present water demand levels and population size or relationship between population size and levels of water scarcity; estimate the future water demand in terms of projected population; and infer the impact of water scarcity on health.

Access to Sources of Drinking Water

The results of the 2000 Population and Housing Census indicate that about 40% of the households in the country have access to pipe-borne water (14% within and 26% outside the households) and tankers provide water to 2% of the households. One third of the households obtain their drinking water from wells and boreholes while the remainder of the households (25%) depend on natural sources such as springs, rain water, rivers, streams, lakes and dugout wells.

Drinking water needs to be of a quality that denotes a tolerable level of risk. The quality of water that is consumed is widely known as an important transmission conduit for infectious diarrhoeal and other diseases. Thus, water produced for direct consumption and ingestion via food should be of a quality that does not pose a significant risk to human life.

Figure 1 shows that a sizeable proportion of households in the country obtains drinking water from unprotected sources. Under normal circumstances, pipe-borne water is regarded as safe for human consumption. What one is not sure of is the extent to which the other sources are well protected. A significant proportion of the households consume water from rivers, streams, lakes, springs and dugout wells, a major health concern. The sources are indicative of a substantial risk to the health of the members of the households. Furthermore, where water supplies are intermittent as a rule rather than an exception, as in many parts of the suburbs in the capital cities and towns, the risk of contaminated water finding its way into the domestic water supplies will escalate. Even where water is supplied through multiple taps in the household, but the supply is intermittent as constantly being experienced in most parts of Accra, a further risk to health may result from mal-functioning of the water borne facilities.

Figure 1 also shows that drinking water is obtained at different levels of service. A quarter of the households have no access to potable water and the members may spend a considerable length of time, say more than thirty minutes, in fetching water. In such a situation, the quantity of water required by the households cannot be secured and hygiene (hand-washing and basic food hygiene) may not be possible and the risk to human life may be high.

Regional and Urban-Rural Differentials

Differential access to sources for drinking water in the various parts of the country is presented in Appendix A

Table 1. Whilst eight and five out of ten households in the Greater Accra and Central Regions respectively have access to pipe-borne water, only between 13 and 15% of the households in the Upper East and Upper West Regions obtain their drinking water from that source. Wells and bore holes are the major sources of drinking water in the latter two regions where between 11 and 13% of the households depend on spring and/or rain water as the major source of drinking water, a situation which may become precarious during the dry season. As a result, a substantial number of the households in the two regions may consume water from unprotected sources (unprotected wells, rivers, streams etc.)

Figure 1. Households by Main Source of drinking Water, 2000 [%]

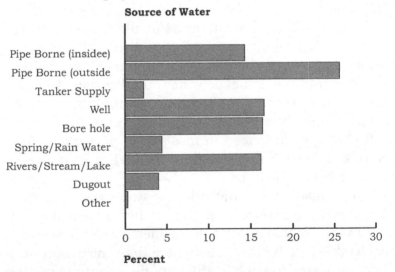

A significant number of households in the remainder of the regions (Western, Volta, Eastern, Ashanti, Brong Ahafo and Northern) draw water for consumption from unprotected sources such as rivers, streams and lakes. Another important feature to note is the comparatively large number of households in the Northern Region, which depend on dugout wells for drinking water. The patterns delineated above underscore various levels of health concerns in the regions.

Majority of the households in the regional capitals have access to pipe-borne water, proportions ranging from 70% in Bolgatanga to 91% in Accra and Takoradi as compared with 53% in Wa. Bolgatanga and Wa depend, to a considerable extent, on wells, bore holes, springs and rain water. Wells are also a major source of drinking water in Koforidua, Ho and Kumasi. Nearly 3% of the households in Sunyani and Tamale obtain their drinking water from rivers, streams and dugout wells.

In most cases, access to pipe-borne water does not mean that the households always secure the required quantity of water. A case in point is the Cape Coast municipality where 98% of the households are reported to have optimal access to treated water but taps are dry for a considerable period of time. The urban-rural differentials are worthy of note. Whilst nearly 68% of the urban households have access to pipe-borne water, only 15% of the rural households draw water from the same source. Nearly six out of ten rural households collect water from wells (17%), bore holes (27%) and rivers, streams and lakes (27%), spring/rain (6.4%) and dugout wells (6.6%).

The effect of water from unprotected sources on health is much more acute among the rural residents than among the urban dwellers though 16% of the urban households depend on wells for domestic water supplies (Figure 2). The unprotected sources such as rivers, streams, lakes, dug-out wells are usually heavily polluted and are mostly responsible for water-borne and water-related diseases such as diarrhoea, cholera, guinea worm, bilharzias, and typhoid that are common among the rural communities. Malaria, diarrhoea and typhoid are reported to be among the ten top causes of morbidity in the country (GSS, 2005).

Population by Access to Main Sources of Water Supply, 1984-2000

The proportion of the population with access to the main sources of water is presented in Table 1. It will be seen from the table that there was no significant change in the proportions of the population with access to pipe borne and bore hole as the main sources of water supply during the sixteen-year period (1984-2000). The proportion with access to pipe borne hovered around 37-38% and that of bore holes stayed close to 37%. The proportion dependent on rivers/streams/lakes declined from 31% to 16% during the period (Figure 3). Notwithstanding, there was very little change in the size of the population with access to those sources, declining slightly from 3.2 million in 1984 to 3.1 million in 2000 (Appendix A Table 2).

On the other hand, the proportions relying on wells, spring/rain water and dugouts climbed up to about 16.6, 4.6 and 4.5% respectively, an indication of a concerted effort being made to provide the communities with relatively more secure sources of water supply (e.g. wells). However, population expansion appears to have compounded the effort as rivers/streams/lakes still remain the main sources of water for a sizeable number of people in the country though the proportion plummeted during the period.

Figure 2. Percent of Households by Main Source of Drinking Water and Residence, 2000

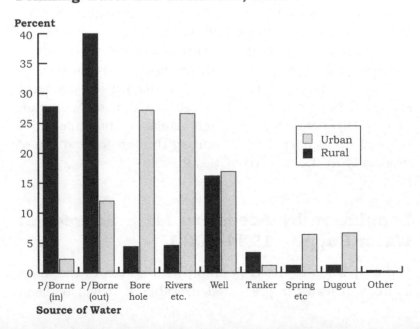

Table1. Percentage of Population with Access to Main Source of Water by Region , 1984-2000

SOURCE	Pipe Borne		Well		Bore Hole		Spring/Rain		River/Stream/Lake		Dugout		Tanker		Other	
REGION	1984	2000	1984	2000	1984	2000	1984	2000	1984	2000	1984	2000	1984	2000	1984*	2000
All Regions	36.6	38.3	11.1	16.6	16.5	17.3	0.5	4.6	31.0	16.3	3.3	4.5	x	2.1	1.0	0.3
Western	32.9	31.7	11.6	23.2	17.0	14.2	0.3	4.3	35.4	24.1	1.5	1.5	x	0.7	1.6	0.3
Central	46.6	50.0	11.3	11.5	12.9	17.3	0.4	2.7	25.4	11.0	2.7	2.4	x	4.9	0.7	0.2
G/Accra	89.0	80.9	4.5	5.4	0.6	1.1	0.1	1.4	4.1	1.6	1.5	1.9	x	7.3	0.2	0.4
Volta	20.8	24.9	19.1	23.0	10.8	9.3	1.5	5.8	44.1	25.7	3.0	10.1	x	0.7	0.7	0.5
Eastern	31.9	28.2	13.4	23.0	14.8	16.5	0.2	5.2	33.9	23.5	4.8	2.8	x	0.6	1.0	0.2
Ashanti	37.9	40.0	6.5	17.5	18.2	22.5	0.3	3.7	34.3	14.1	1.5	1.3	x	0.7	1.3	0.2
B/Ahafo	26.1	23.1	12.1	15.3	8.6	26.5	0.9	5.5	45.8	25.8	4.7	3.1	x	0.6	1.8	0.1
Northern	21.4	22.4	17.8	12.6	20.0	17.0	0.3	4.4	49.0	22.8	8.6	19.6	x	0.9	0.9	0.3
Upper East	13.3	13.2	11.3	31.6	63.6	36.6	0.8	10.7	8.2	4.5	2.0	2.6	x	0.5	0.8	0.3
Upper West	15.1	15.5	1.7	10.6	68.1	47.8	0.2	13.1	9.3	7.6	4.6	4.5	x	0.6	1.0	0.3

Source; 1984 and 2000 Population and Housing Censuses, GSS

Population Growth, Water/Sanitation and Health

Although the proportion of the population with access to unprotected sources declined from 45.5% in 1984 to 42% in 2000, there is still a huge population which fetches water from unsafe sources; rising from 5.6 million in 1984 to 8.0 million in 2000 (Table 2).

The regional differentials indicate that apart from the Central Region, there were significant increases in the size of the populations with access to unprotected sources. The percentage increase ranges from 10.3% in the Greater Accra Region to 99% in the Upper East Region (Table 2). The decline of the proportion of the population with access to pipe borne water in the Greater Accra Region and the increase in the proportion dependent on wells during the sixteen-year period is also indicative of the impact of the expansion of the region's population on the provision of safe water to its inhabitants. The continual intermittency of water supply in the region's capital may be attributable, among other things, to the rapid rise of its population over the years and inadequate resources to meet the needs of the increasing population. It is the region with the fastest growing population in the country, expanding at the rate of 4.4% per year during the period under review (1984-2000).

In the Volta Region, though there was five percentage points increase in the proportion with access to pipe borne water, dugout wells became a major source of water supply for 10% of the population, the second highest in the country after the Northern Region where about 20% of the population draw most of the required water from that source. In the Eastern and Brong Ahafo Regions, the proportions with access to pipe borne water declined and there was virtually no significant changes in Ashanti, Northern, Upper East and Upper West Regions where the proportions dependent on wells rather increased significantly except in the Northern Region whose major sources include dugout wells.

In the Upper East and Upper West Regions, the proportion of the population with access to bore hole substantially declined during the period and as already pointed out, the trend towards wells and spring/rain water accelerated. On the other hand, there was a tremendous increase in the proportion depending on bore holes as the main source of water in the Brong Ahafo Region, rising from about 9% in 1984 to 27% in 2000.

Overall, there was no significant increase in the proportion of the population with access to pipe borne and bore hole as the main source of water supply except in the Brong Ahafo Region where reliance on the latter surged. Secondly, the proportion depending on wells rose substantially in all regions except in the Central and Northern Regions where 5% of the population of the Central Region relied on tanker truck provision (the second highest in the country after Greater Accra Region- 7%) and dugout wells as the main source for 20% of residents in the Northern Region (Table 1). Although the proportion depending on surface water dropped considerably in most of the regions, it is the only source of water for 3.1 million Ghanaians and wells, spring/rain water and dugout wells are the source for another 4.9 million; 6.3 million of the 8 million Ghanaians with access to unprotected water reside in the rural areas as shown in Table 2.

Population expansion appears to pose a huge challenge of providing adequate and clean water to Ghanaian communities. Regions experiencing comparatively high growth rates such as Greater Accra (4.4%), Ashanti (3.4%), Northern (2.8%) and Brong Ahafo (2.5%) made very little progress in providing clean water to their inhabitants and in some cases, the proportion with access to clean or safe water declined (for example, Greater Accra, Eastern and Brong Ahafo).

Even in high-income countries, purely technical solutions mitigate only some of the demand for water. In the long term, slowing population growth and effectively implementing policies and programmes for improved water management are key to sustainable development. Thus unless policy-makers, decision-makers as well as water management specialists seriously integrate demographic trends into development programmes, all efforts to meet increasing demand for water will fail.

Figure 3. Population with Access to Main Source of Water [%] 1984-2000

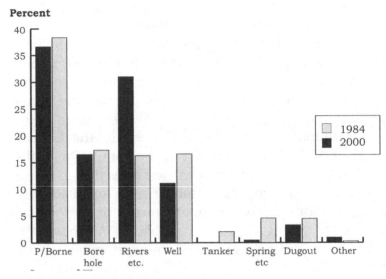

Table 2. Population with Access to Unprotected* Water by Region and Residence, 2000

Region	1984	2000	% Increase	Urban	Rural
Western	566382	1023368	80.7	198835	824533
Central	454779	443999	-0.02	102026	341973
G/Accra	146014	296478	10.3	152129	144349
Volta	820934	1049681	27.9	223068	826613
Eastern	877833	1148582	30.8	279783	868799
Ashanti	860202	1323360	53.8	492063	831297
B/Ahafo	766435	915406	19.4	256661	658745
Northern	881702	1079256	22.4	133003	946253
Upper East	171661	513453	99.1	106644	406809
Upper West	69347	184643	66.3	736	183907
All Regions	5647289	7978226	41.3	1944948	6299086

Source: 2000 Population and Housing Census, Ghana Statistical Service (GSS).

* Include unprotected wells and spring, rivers, streams and lakes, excluding tanker truck provision which may be unprotected (14.9% and 4.9% of households in the Greater Accra and Central Regions respectively depend on this source for drinking water).

Quantity and Quality of Water Required to Promote Good Health

The need for domestic water supplies for basic health protection exceeds the minimum required for drinking and cooking. Though there is no information on the quantity of water required for cooking, one may assume that the quantity needed for both drinking and cooking is collected at the same time from the same source. Nevertheless, additional volumes of water are required for hygiene (maintenance of personal hygiene through hand and foot washing and laundry). Poor hygiene may be attributable, in part, to lack of sufficient quantity of domestic water supply. Diseases linked to poor hygiene include diarrhoeal and other diseases transmitted through faecal-anal route as well as diseases related to infestation (e.g. louse and tick-borne typhoid).

Lack of access to safe and adequate water supplies contributes to ongoing poverty through economic cost of poor health, the need to purchase water (affordability) and time and energy expended in collecting water in poor communities. One may glean from Figures 1 and 2 and Tables 1 and 2 that the water consumed by a sizeable proportion of the population is obtained from unprotected sources such as wells, rivers, streams and lakes. As already pointed out, the quality of water that is consumed is widely recognised as an important conduit for infectious diseases. It also plays a vital role in epidemic and contributes to endemic diseases from pathogens.

There are therefore strong links between water supply, hygiene and disease. Contaminated water and lack of adequate quantities of water for personal hygiene give rise to water-borne and water-washed diseases such as infectious hepatitis, diarrhoeal diseases, typhoid, and guinea worm. Thus, water, hygiene and diseases are linked to sanitation. The data collected in the 2000 census on disposal of solid and liquid waste and toilet facilities throw some light on the linkages.

Sanitation: Disposal of Solid and Liquid Waste

The country is saddled with the problem of indiscriminate solid waste disposal and this has given rise to pollution of water bodies and exposure of the populace to numerous health threats. Nearly 58% of the households dump their solid waste at designated dumping sites while 25% deposit it ubiquitously (Figure 4). Only about 5% of the households pay for their solid waste to be collected while nearly 8 and 4% respectively burn or bury it. Management of solid waste in the country seems to be chaotic. The regions exhibit a fairly similar pattern except in the three northern regions where majority of the households abandon solid waste far and wide.

In the regional capitals, the proportion of households which dump the waste at the designated sites range from 62% in Accra and 63% in Tamale to 81% in Cape Coast and 82% in Kumasi. A significant proportion of the households in Bolgatanga (28%) and Wa (29%) deposit the waste outside the designated sites. Even in the nation's capital, only 21% of the households pay for the solid waste to be collected. The likelihood of dumping the waste indiscriminately is greater among the rural households than in the urban areas where 67% of the households take it to the public site and 8% pay for it to be collected. All told, solid waste is not properly disposed off in the country and the probability of the environment becoming increasingly polluted is pretty high.

Haphazard disposal of liquid waste and poor drainage systems have given rise to water logging and stagnant pools, which pose threat to the health of the communities. Nearly 95% of the households dispose of liquid waste onto streets, gutters or compounds and only about 5% of the households utilize sewerage system (Figure 5). The pattern is repeated in the regions except in Brong Ahafo and the three northern regions where gutters do not feature significantly and this may be attributed to a limited number of them in the cities and towns as well as in the rural areas. Streets and compounds are therefore the major recipients of liquid waste.

Figure 4. Households by Solid Waste Disposal and Residence, 2000 [%]

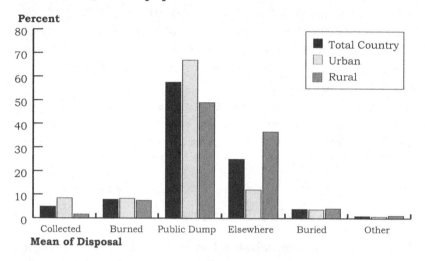

Figure 5. Households by Liquid Waste Disposal and Residence [%] 2000

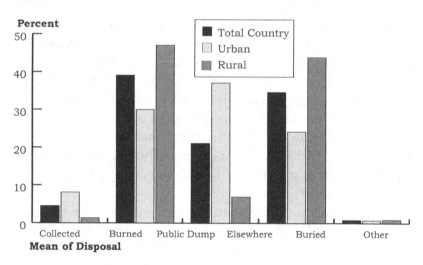

The regional capitals portray a virtually similar pattern except that comparatively higher proportions of the households discharge the liquid waste into the sewerage system, ranging between 9% in Kumasi to 13% in Accra. In the urban areas, about 91% of the households dispose of the liquid waste onto streets, gutter and compounds while 91% of the rural households throw it onto streets and compounds since gutters are non-existent in many areas. Thus, in both urban and rural areas, large volumes of water are left to either evaporate or become stagnant, polluting the atmosphere and creating congenial conditions for mosquitoes and other communicable disease agents to breed and, in consequence, pose serious threats to human life.

In a nutshell, the mode of disposal of both solid and liquid wastes is inimical to the health of the people and would eventually lead to increases in the levels of morbidity and mortality.

Access to Toilet Facility

One-fifth of the households have no access to toilet facilities and members are therefore presumed to defecate in the nearby bush or on the beach. One-third of the households use public toilets while 22% have access to pit latrines. It appears that one of the major factors that restrict the use of modern facility (i.e. water closet) is water availability; only 9% of the households have access to this facility. However, in the Greater Accra Region as well as in the regional capitals, the proportions using the modern facility are comparatively higher, ranging from 22% in Koforidua and 23% in Accra metropolis to 33% in Cape Coast. But in view of constant water shortages in the cities, effective use of this facility to promote good hygiene may be limited.

One of the worrying features reflected in the census figures is that between seven and eight out of ten households in the three northern regions have no toilet facilities and only about 3 per cent use a water closet (Figure 6). The proportions of the households in their capitals using this facility are the lowest in the country, ranging between 9% in Tamale and Wa to 15 per cent in Bolgatanga. And the highest proportions with no toilet facility are found in Bolgatanga (40%), Wa (28%) and Tamale (19%) [see also Appendix B Tables 1 and 2].

In the rural areas, less than 2% of the households

have access to water closet and majority of them (31%) use pit latrine while 28% have no toilet facility. In the urban areas, 37% of the households use the public toilets and 12% have access to pit latrines, while 11% of the households presumably defecate on the beach or in the bush (Figure 7). Pollution of the atmosphere and water bodies, particularly in the urban areas and the resultant threat to health cannot be overemphasised.

Figure 6. Percent of Households by Toilet Facility and Region, 2000

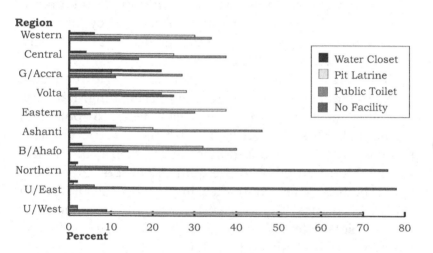

Figure 7. Percent of Households by Toilet Facility and Residence, 2000

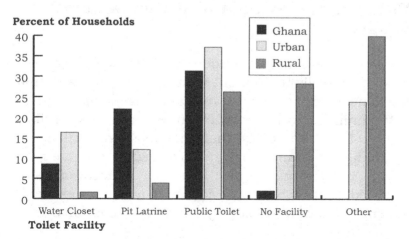

Impact of Pollution on Health

Pollution in the urban areas is reported to be mainly organic in nature and it stems from domestic wastes, particularly sewage and garbage. The improper solid and liquid waste disposal practices have affected the bacteriological quality of water bodies. The main threat to human health from water pollution is through ingestion of contaminated water and food as well as using it for personal hygiene, agriculture, industry, recreation and by living near water bodies. Microbiological agents (e.g. bacteria, viruses etc) are, to a large extent, responsible for the diarrhoeal morbidity and mortality that take a heavy toll, especially among children. They are also responsible for gastro-intestinal disorders and cholera (Gyau-Boakye et. al. 2002).

Pollution in the rural areas is localized and restricted to centres of activities like mining and farming. Farming activities in the rural areas can lead to pollution (through the use of fertilizers and pesticides), erosion, sedimentation, and siltation of rural rivers and reservoirs, which reduce both the quantity and quality of the water bodies. These activities impact on the quality of the water bodies. Consequently, high chloride and suspended solids levels are found in many rivers in the country (Gyau-Boakye et al. 2002).

Future Population and Water Demand Levels

The available evidence underscores two major issues. Firstly, accessibility influences the quantity of water that the households collect; distance and time being the main determining factors. Nearly six in ten households collect water at service levels that may pose difficulties in obtaining the quantity of water required to promote good health. Reliability may also influence quantity of water collected. Although direct evidence may be non-existent, intermittency of water supply, which is a common occurrence in most cities and towns, is an indication that reliability may influence quantity of water. Cost may also affect quantity of water, particularly in the poor rural communities and the poor urban suburbs.

Secondly, the water that is consumed by four out of ten households or by 8 million Ghanaians is obtained from unprotected sources that are indicative of a substantial risk to health. Provision of potable and safe water in the country is therefore riddled by problems relating to quantity and quality.

Notwithstanding, a major challenge is the provision of ample quantity of water required for direct consumption, hygiene, laundry and bathing in light of the sustained population growth which places severe constraints on water availability to achieve development goals.

Surface Water Availability

We attempt to assess the amount of water available for use in the river systems, estimate the percentage of the overall availability that can be made accessible for withdrawal, determine the relationship between present water demand levels and population size and estimate the future water demand in terms of projected population and infer the impact of water scarcity on health.

The Water Research Institute has since the 1970s divided the river basins of Ghana into three broad systems on the basis of the climate and other factors. These are the South-Western Rivers System, which is composed of Pra, Ankobra, Tano and Bia rivers; the Coastal Rivers System, which includes the Kakum, Ochi-Amisa, Ochi-Nakwa, Ayensu, Densu and Tordzie rivers; and the Volta Rivers System, made up of the Red, Black and White and the Oti rivers. The Volta Rivers System covers about 70% of the country and contributes about 64.7% of the actual runoff from Ghana. Table 3– presents data on rainfall in the three basin systems in the country. The South-Western Rivers System covers about 22% of Ghana and contributes 29.2% of the actual runoff, while the Coastal Rivers System covers about 8% of the country and contributes 6.1% of the actual runoff. The total annual runoff from Ghana alone is 54.4 billion m^3 of which the runoff from Ghana alone is 39.4 billion m^3, representing 68.6% of the total annual runoff. The remaining 15.0 billion m^3 originates from outside Ghana's territory (WARM, 1998).

Table3: Mean Annual Rainfall and Runoff Variabilities in the Volta, South-Western and Coastal Basin Systems

Basin System	Mean Annual Rainfall Range (mm)	Coefficient of Mean Annual Rainfall Variability %	Coefficient of Variation of Mean Annual Runoff %
Basin System	876-1500	15-20	13-63
South Western	1216-2000	17-32	17-63
Coastal	774-1700	20-34	11-66

Source: WARM (1998).

The mean annual internal runoffs for the Volta, South-Western and Coastal Systems are given by WARM (1998) as 24,175, 13,125 and 2,110 million m^3 respectively. Tables 4-8 show the dynamics of water available per capita in the basins from 2000 to 2025. The runoff figures used to determine the water availability per capita are the mean annual runoffs. It must be noted that these runoffs have coefficient of variation ranging from 11 to 66% (see Table 3).

The per capita water availability values presented in Tables 4-7 may be better understood if they are assessed in relation to the most widely used measure (i.e. Falkenmark indicator or Water Stress Index). When water supply falls below 1,700 m^3, 1,000 m^3 and 500 m^3 , a country is said to be experiencing ware stress, water scarcity and absolute scarcity respectively (Falkenmark, Lundqvist and Widstrand 1989).

Table 4: Dynamics of Water Availability per capita (m^3/person) in the Volta, South-Western and Coastal Basins (2000-2025)

Basin System		Volta	South West	Coastal	Total
2000	Population	7,318,974	6,354,458	5,238,648	18,912,080
	Water Availability per capita	3,303	2,065	403	2,084
2005	Population	8,263.590	7,058,923	5,841,987	21,134,500
	Water Availability per capita	2,925	1,859	361	1,865
2010	Population	9,266,229	7,811,783	6,380,796	23,458,808
	Water Availability per capita	2.609	1,680	331	1,680
2015	Population	10,354,110	8,615,450	6,980,590	25,950,150
	Water Availability per capita	2,335	1,523	302	1,519
2020	Population	11,518,779	9,380,391	7,612,658	28,511,828
	Water Availability per capita	2,099	1,399	277	1,382
2025	Population	12,806,376	10,238,838	8,266,218	31,311,432
	Water Availability per capita	1,888	1,282	255	1,259

109

Table 5 Volta Basin

Year	Population	Maximum Availability of Water (cubic per capita per year)		
		Achievable Level of Use		
		100 percent	20 percent	30 percent
2000	7,318,974	3303	661	991
2005	8,263,590	2925	585	878
2010	9,266,229	2609	522	783
2015	10,354,110	2335	467	700
2020	11,518,779	2099	420	630
2025	12,806,376	1888	378	566

Table 6 South-Western Basin

Year	Population	Maximum Availability of Water (cubic per capita per year)		
		Achievable Level of Use		
		100 percent	20 percent	30 percent
2000	6,354,458	2065	413	620
2005	7,058,923	1859	372	558
2010	7,811,783	1680	336	504
2015	8,615,450	1525	305	457
2020	9,380,391	1399	280	420
2025	10,238,838	1282	256	386

Table 7a Coastal Basin

Year	Population	Maximum Availability of Water (cubic per capita per year)		
		Achievable Level of Use		
		100 percent	20 percent	30 percent
2000	5238,648	403	81	121
2005	5,841,987	361	72	108
2010	6,380,796	331	66	99
2015	6,980,590	302	60	91
2020	7,612,658	277	55	83
2025	8,266,218	255	51	77

Table 7b Coastal [Accra Metropolis]

Year	Population	Maximum Availability of Water (cubic per capita per year)		
		Achievable Level of Use		
		100 percent	20 percent	30 percent
2000	1,658,937	1,273	255	382
2005	1,943,127	1,086	217	326
2010	2,262,794	933	187	280
2015	2,617,962	806	161	245
2020	3,007,210	702	140	215
2025	3,427,461	615	123	185

Appraisal of the data presented in the tables in terms of Falkenmark indicator or water Stress Index indicates that:

(i) Assuming 100% achievable level of use (using all the available water in the basin), the Volta System will experience water stress after 2025, whereas the South-Western System is currently experiencing water stress conditions.

(ii) The Coastal Basin is presently experiencing absolute scarcity conditions with the maximum water availability of 403 cubic meters in 2000 decreasing to 361 cubic meters in 2005 and it is expected to decline to 302 in 2015 and then to 255 in 2025 as a result of rapid population expansion.

According to Falkenmark (1990), 100% of the total water flow is seldom possible to mobilise, especially in hot and flat countries. Where topographical constraints make water storage difficult, or where a hot climate causes large losses of stored water due to evaporation, it may be difficult to raise the water mobilisation level above 20 or 30%.

It will be seen from Tables 6-8 that with 20 or 30% of water mobilisation, all the basin systems - Volta, South-Western and Coastal - are presently experiencing water scarcity conditions. Thus, even with 30% achievable level of use, the whole of Ghana is experiencing severe water scarcity conditions at the moment. The extent of water scarcity increases with continued population growth. The situation is much more acute in the coastal areas where water availability per capita is much lower compared to that in the other basins; water availability per capita of 121 cubic metres in 2000 declined to 108 in 2005 and it is expected to fall to 77 cubic metres by the end of the first quarter of this century (Table 7a). In fact, Coastal areas are presently experiencing absolute scarcity and the situation worsens as the population expands. The fastest growing region (Greater Accra) in the country is located in the coastal basin. The population of this region expanded at the annual growth rate of 4.4% during the period 1984 - 2000. It is therefore not surprising that water is rationed and the inhabitants are currently living through absolute water scarcity. South-Western basin will encounter absolute scarcity by 2010.

The gravity of population pressure on available water may be gleaned from the relationship between water demand levels and the projected population of the Accra metropolis. Even if the entire available water in the coastal basin is mobilized for the exclusive use of the inhabitants of the metropolis, absolute scarcity conditions will still persist. The degree of scarcity (measured by the number of persons per unit of water flow) escalates with population expansion (Table 7b). As noted above, mobilisation of 100% of the total water flow is hardly ever achieved and it is even difficult to raise the mobilisation level above 20 or 30%. It will be seen from Table 7b that the city dwellers will experience severe water conditions in the coming years. The need to plan to transfer large volumes of water to the coastal basin cannot therefore be overemphasized.

The pressure of population expansion on available water is also highlighted by the rapid population expansion in the cities and towns. The cities and towns which experienced high percentage increase of their populations between 1984 and 2000 include the following:

- Kumawu (86 %) in the Main Volta Basin
- Dambae (122 %), and Bambilla (95%) in the Oti River Basin
- Kuraga (120 %) and Walewale (72%) in the White river basin
- Kintampo (103%) and WA (85%) in the Black River Basin
- Bibiani (120%) in the Ankobra River Basin
- Foso (111%), Asokore (71%), Konongo ((95%), Kumasi (136%) and Obuasi (91%) in the Pra River Basin
- Techiman (122%), Odumase (81%), Nsuatre (94%), Goaso (95%) and Mim (70%) in the Tano River Basin
- Accra (91%), Ashiama (195%), Madina (170%), Nungua (116%) and Tema New Town (214%) in the Coastal Basin
- Akatsi (205), Aflao (77%) and Ho (63%) in the Todzie-Aka Basin.

The chronic intermittency and severe water scarcity being experienced by the cities and towns is a clear indication of the extent to which water demand levels greatly outstrip water supply as a result of intense population pressure. Analysis of water availability in the regional capitals and the Greater Accra Region throws much light on the quantitative dimensions of the water problem in the urban communities.

Domestic Water Demand

Urban Water Supply
The Ghana Water Company Limited (GWCL) adopts 90 litres per capita per day as water consumption design criterion for the urban communities. Based on this requirement, production data obtained from GWCL are utilized in assessing the extent to which the estimated increasing demand levels in the coming years could be

met. The estimated daily requirements of water for the regional capitals and the Greater Accra Region are presented in Table 8. An average daily production ranges from 720,000 litres in Bolgatanga to 365,809,000 litres in the Greater Accra Region. It will be seen from the table that the estimated levels of demand far exceed that of production except in Greater Accra Region where the demand is currently slightly below the production level. The demand levels are about twice as high as the production levels in Sekondi/Takoradi, Cape Coast, Kumasi, Sunyani, Tamale and Bolgatanga and nearly three times as high in Koforidua. Wa exhibits a more serious scenario where the demand exceeds production by nearly ten times. The escalating population pressure on water resources is depicted by the projected estimates for the next decade (i.e. 2005-2015). The estimates indicate that unless production is substantially increased in the coming years, it is very unlikely that the projected water demand could be met during the projection period. The 90 litres per capita per day design criterion has not therefore been realized with the existing installed capacities in the various urban centres. Nevertheless, for the purpose of strategic planning, an assessment of the actual water availability for domestic consumption in these urban areas has been carried out.

In view of the loss due to leakages and other factors during the production process and proportion of water consumed by industrial and commercial establishments, the actual water available for domestic consumption is much less than the total production. The quantity of water lost in the production process is estimated to range between 45 and 50%[4] in Greater Accra Region to between 30 and 35% in the regional capitals. Proportion of water consumed by industries and commercial entities ranges from between 20 and 30% in Greater Accra Region, Kumasi and Sekondi/Takoradi and between 5 and 20% in the other capitals[5]. The quantity of water available for domestic consumption in each capital is therefore computed on the basis of these estimates. The derived amount of water for use by each urban dweller in a day is shown in Table 9. The quantity of water potentially available to serve the urban dwellers is much less than the GWCL estimated demand of 90 litres per capita per person; ranging from about 7 litres per capita per day in Bolgatanga to 40 litres in the Greater Accra Region. The dwindling quantity of water available for use by each person in a day between 2005 and 2015 is indicative of population pressure. Table 9 also depicts various levels of water scarcity that is being experienced by the urban communities. Overall, the available data indicate that levels of demand far exceed that of supply. The huge gap between demand and supply therefore poses a big challenge towards the achievement of water related millennium development goals.

Rural Water Supply

Rural communities rely mainly on rivers, streams, ponds, springs, rain water and lakes for their water supply. Most of these sources are polluted and they are the main sources of water-borne diseases, which are so common in the rural areas. A sizeable number of the rivers and streams are not perennial and the rural communities cannot therefore depend on them for their water requirements throughout the year. Likewise, rainfall harvesting cannot be undertaken throughout the year as a result of the pattern of rainfall.

There is therefore the need to find alternative sources of sustainable water supply for the rural communities. Groundwater has been found to be a reliable source of water both in terms of quantity and quality for the rural communities. Consequently, the percentage of the rural residents who depend on boreholes and wells has been rising substantially since 1984. In 1986, about 7,800 bore holes were drilled in the various geological formations and 9,500 hand-dug wells were constructed (Gyau-Boakye 2001).

In 1998, Community Water and Sanitation Agency (CWSA) was mandated by an Act of Parliament to facilitate the provision of safe drinking water and related sanitation services to rural communities and small towns in the country. At the time of writing, CWSA was operating in all the ten regions, 109 districts and 12, 672 communities. As of March 1998, 11,500 bore holes had been drilled throughout the country and 60,000 hand-dug wells had been constructed, providing sources of water to about 52% of the rural population as compared with 41% in 1984 (Gyawu-Boakye 1999). The 2000 census results indicate that 44% of the rural population depends on groundwater (i.e. bore holes and wells). According to CWSA, the national coverage for potable water supply in both rural communities and small towns was 46% in 2004 (CWSA 2004). The available statistics show that during the ten-year period,(1994-2004), 13,196 bore holes and 1,344 hand-dug out wells were constructed and were providing additional sources of water to rural communities.

The available information therefore indicates that the national coverage for potable water supply in the rural communities increased from 41% in 1984 to 52% in 1998 and declined to 44% in 2000. In 2004, 46%[6] of the rural communities and small towns had access to bore holes and/or hand-dugout wells. In view of the concerted efforts being made by CWSA to provide the rural communities with potable water, the inability to cover the rural areas is mostly attributable to population expansion. The rural population rose from 8.4 million in 1984 to 10.6 million in 2000, growing at an annual growth rate of 1.6%. And it is projected to climb up to 11.6 million in 2015.

Table 8. Water Supply Systems By Regional Capitals 2000-2015

Region/Regional Capitals	Installed Capacity (m³/d)	Current Production (litres per day)	Daily Water Demand (Litres)			
			2000	2005	2010	2015
Sekondi-Takoradi	n/a	14,335,000	26,063,370	26,741,430	26,929,980	26,994,960
CapeCoast &Environs	31,700	13,763,000	23,490,180	25,121,790	26,026,830	26,503,830
G/Accra	1,928,505	365,809,000	261,515,340	319,173,210	385,522,020	463,132,260
Ho &Environs	18,000	6,628,000	21,179,790	21,690,450	22,008,240	22,203,000
Koforidua & Environs	5,430	4,337,000	11,927,610	12,937,770	13,838,580	14,620,950
Kumasi	81,818	64,775,000	105,324,300	146,292,210	181,945,620	204,456,870
Sunyani & Environs	6,800	6,901,000	13,177,710	15,283,980	17,541,360	19,908,720
Tamale & Environs	19,400	14,046,000	22,430,160	25,846,110	29,111,400	32,097,870
Bolga & Environs	6,000	2,031,000	4,424,580	4,913,910	5,852,880	6,283,260
Wa & Environs	2,800	720,000	5,997,968	6,919,650	7,509,510	7,805,520

Population Growth, Water/Sanitation and Health

Table 9. Population and Per Capita Water Demand By Regional capitals 2000-2015

Region/Regional Capital	Population and Water Availability for Domestic Consumption (litres per capita per day)							
	2000		2005		2010		2015	
	Population	l/c/d	Population	l/c/d	Population	l/c/d	Population	l/c/d
Sekondi-Takoradi	289,593	22.3	297,127	22.0	299,222	21.0	299,944	20.0
Cape Coast *	261,002	31.6	279,131	29.0	289,187	28.5	294,487	28.0
G/Accra	2,905,726	49.2	3,546,369	40.0	4,283,578	33.0	5,145,914	28.0
Ho *	235,331	23.5	241,005	17.9	244,536	17.6	246,700	17.4
Koforidua*	132,529	21.3	143,753	19.6	153,762	18.3	162,455	17.0
Kumasi Metropolis	1,170,270	22.1	1,625,469	15.9	2,021,618	12.8	2,271,743	11.4
Sunyan*	146,419	30.6	169,822	26.4	194,904	23.0	221,208	20.3
Tamale *	249,224	36.6	287,179	31.8	323,460	28.2	356,643	25.6
Bolgatanga *	49,162	31.0	54,599	27.9	65,032	23.3	69,184	22.0
Wa *	66,644	8.1	66,644	7.0	74,787	6.5	81,494	6.2

* The installations serve surrounding communities as well.

The rural population is split into three groups in accordance with size of community as delineated by CWSA on the basis of required technology and cost estimates (CWSA 2004). It will be seen from Table 10 that majority of the rural residents live in communities with a population size of between 300 and 2,000 inhabitants. The population of these communities rose from 3.5 million in 1970 to 5.5 million in 2000. The fastest growing population is that of the largest communities (i.e. 2,000-5,000 inhabitants), the annual growth rate shot up from 3.2 in 1970-1984 to 4.4% in 1984-2000. The population of the smallest communities (i.e. 75-300 inhabitants) increased by only 6.6% in sixteen years (1984-2000); the annual rate of growth plummeted to 0.4% during that period (Table 10).

Table 10 Rural Population by Community Size

Size of Community	1970	1984	2000
75-300	1,575,724	1,938,230	2,067,579
301-2000	3,491,712	4,642,444	5,536,670
2001-5000	958,068	1,519,543	2,915,220
Total	6,026,504	8,100,217	10,519,469

Intercensal Growth Rate [%]

	1970-1984	1984-2000
75-300	1.5	0.4
301-2000	2.0	1.1
2001-5000	3.2	4.4

Per Cent of Rural Population

	1970	1984	2000
75-300	26.1	23.9	19.7
301-2000	57.9	57.3	52.6
2001-5000	16.0	18.8	27.7
Total	100.0	100.0	100.0

Projected Population

	2005	2010	2015
75-300	2,101,008	2,058,429	1,990,694
301-2000	5,783,304	5,845,470	5,844,266
2001-5000	3,173,630	3,468, 615	3,738,844
Total	11,057,942	11,372,509	11,573,804

Thus, the bulk of the rural population is located in the communities with population size of between 301 and 2,000 inhabitants. The population of these communities is expected increase to 5.8 million within the next decade. The recommended technology for providing water to these communities is the drilling of bore holes, which are reported to be expensive to install and the foreign currency component of the cost is huge (Gyau-Boakye 2001). Furthermore, it has been observed that due to geological limitations, it is not everywhere that groundwater is available or available in the required quantities. Some of the rural communities will therefore have to rely solely on surface water resources whilst others have to resort to the use of both surface and ground water as occurring in certain towns and villages.

Hand-dug well facility is recommended for the communities with a population size of between 75 and 300. Though out-migration has substantially slowed down the expansion of the population, 2 million people live in these communities which are scattered throughout the country. To provide all of them with clean drinking water is a difficult undertaking, to say the least. The estimated population indicates that over 7,000 hand-dug wells need to be constructed within the coming decade. Population pressure on the pipe system for the largest communities (i.e. 2,001-5,000 inhabitants) may be inferred from Table 10. Population expansion will play a critical role in the provision of adequate water to these communities. The rapid population growth implies that the proportion of the population with access to water may decrease over time unless the pace of expansion of coverage is accelerated or at least maintained.

To achieve 100% coverage of the rural population by 2015 will require a huge financial investment. Provision of adequate and clean drinking water for promotion of sustainable good health and reduction of deaths caused by water-borne and related diseases among the rural communities will require a great effort in terms of financial investment and technology to ensure access to, at least, basic level service in all rural areas by 2015.

Summary and Policy Implications

Summary

Household, Population and Main Source of Water Supply
The 2000 Population and Housing Census results indicate that about 40% of the households in the country have access to pipe-borne water (14% within and 26% outside the households). One third of the households obtain their drinking water from wells and bore holes whilst the remainder of the households (25%) depend on natural sources such as springs, rain water, rivers, streams, lakes and dugout wells. Thus, a significant proportion of the households consume water from sources which are indicative of a substantial risk to the health of the members of the households. The households fetching water at the two service levels (58%)[7] are most likely to experience difficulties in obtaining adequate water to promote good health.

While eight and five out of 10 households in the Greater Accra and Central Regions respectively have access to pipe-borne water, only between 13 and 15% of the households in the Upper East and Upper West Regions obtain their drinking water from that source. Wells and bore holes are the major sources of drinking water in the Upper East and Upper West Regions. A sizeable number of households in the remainder of the regions (Western, Volta, Eastern, Ashanti, Brong Ahafo and Northern) draw water for consumption from unprotected sources such as rivers, streams and lakes.

Majority of the households in the regional capitals have access to pipe-borne water. Bolgatanga and Wa depend, to a considerable extent, on wells, bore holes, springs and rain water. Wells are also a major source of drinking water in Koforidua, Ho and Kumasi. Nearly 3% of the households in Sunyani and Tamale obtain their drinking water from rivers, streams and dugout wells. Sixty-eighty percent of the urban households have access to pipe-borne water as compared with only 15% of the rural households. Nearly six out of ten rural households collect water from wells (17%), bore holes

(27%) and rivers, streams and lakes (27%), spring/rain (6.4%) and dugout wells (6.6%).

Results of the 1984 and 2000 censuses show that there was no significant increase in the proportion of the population with access to pipe borne and bore bole as the main source of water supply though in absolute terms, the population with access to pipe borne water increased from 4.5 million to 7.2 million during the sixteen year period.

The proportion depending on wells rose substantially in all regions except in the Central and Northern Regions where 5% and 20% of the populations respectively depend on tanker truck provision and dugout well as the main sources of water. Although the proportion depending on surface water (i.e. rivers, streams and lakes) dropped considerably in most of the regions, it is still the only source of water for 3.1million Ghanaians and wells, spring/rain water and dugout wells are the sources of water for another 4.9 million; 6.3 million of the 8 million Ghanaians with access to unprotected water reside in the rural areas.

Population expansion therefore poses a huge challenge of providing Ghanaian communities with adequate and clean water. Regions experiencing comparatively high growth rates such as Greater Accra (4.4%), Ashanti (3.4%), Northern (2.8%) and Brong Ahafo (2.5%) made very little progress in providing clean water to their inhabitants and in some cases, the proportion with access to clean or safe water declined (as particularly found in Greater Accra, Eastern and Brong Ahafo Regions).

The available information indicates that additional volumes of water are required for hygiene (maintenance of personal hygiene through hand and food washing and laundry). Poor hygiene may be attributable, in part, to lack of sufficient quantity of domestic water supply. Diseases linked to poor hygiene include diarrhoeal and other diseases transmitted through faecal-anal route as well as diseases related to infestation (e.g. louse and tick-borne typhoid).

Lack of access to safe and adequate water supplies contributes to ongoing poverty through economic cost of poor health, the need to purchase water (affordability) and time and energy expended in collecting water in poor communities. The quality of water that is consumed is widely recognised as an important conduit for infectious diseases. It also plays a vital role in epidemic and contributes to endemic diseases from pathogens.

There are therefore strong links between water supply, hygiene and disease. Contaminated or polluted water and lack of adequate quantities of water for personal hygiene give rise to water-borne and water-washed diseases such as infectious hepatitis, diarrhoeal diseases, typhoid, and guinea worm. The data collected in the 2000 census on disposal of solid and liquid waste and toilet facilities throw some light on the linkages between water, hygiene, disease, and sanitation.

Solid and Liquid Waste Disposal
Nearly 58% of the households dump their solid waste at designated dumping sites while 25% deposit it ubiquitously. Only about 5% of the households pay for their solid waste to be collected. The regions exhibit a fairly similar pattern except in the three northern regions where majority of the households abandon solid waste far and wide.

In the nation's capital, Accra, only 21% of the households pay for the solid waste to be collected. The likelihood of dumping the waste far and wide is greater among the rural households than in the urban areas where 67% of the households take it to the public site and 8 per cent pay for it to be collected. Solid waste is not properly disposed off in this country and the probability of the environment becoming polluted is very high.

Haphazard disposal of liquid waste and poor drainage systems have given rise to water logging and stagnant pools, which pose threat to the health of the communities. Nearly 95% of the households dispose of liquid waste onto streets, gutters or compounds and only about 5% of the households utilize sewerage system.

Both the regions and their capitals portray a virtually similar pattern. In both urban and rural areas large volumes of water are left to either evaporate or become stagnant, polluting the atmosphere and creating congenial conditions for mosquitoes and other communicable disease agents to breed and, in consequence, pose serious threats to human life. The mode of disposal of both solid and liquid wastes is inimical to the health of the people and would eventually lead to increases in the levels of morbidity and mortality.

Toilet Facility
One-fifth of the households have no access to toilet facilities and members therefore defecate in the nearby bush or on the beach. One third of the households use public toilets while 22% have access to pit latrines. In the Greater Accra Region as well as in the regional capitals, the proportions using the modern facility are comparatively higher, ranging from 22% in Koforidua, 23 in Accra to 33% in Cape Coast. But in view of constant water shortages in the cities, effective use of this facility to promote good hygiene may be limited.

Between seven and eight out of ten households in the three northern regions have no toilet facilities and only about 3% use a water closet. In the rural areas, less than 2% of the households have access to water closet and 28% have no toilet facility as compared with 16 and 11% in the urban areas respectively. Pollution of the atmosphere and water bodies, particularly in the urban areas and the resultant threat to health cannot be overemphasised.

Future Population and Water Demand Levels
The available evidence underscores two major issues. Firstly, accessibility influences the quantity of water that the households collect; distance and time being the main determining factors. Nearly six in 10 households collect water at service levels that may pose difficulties in obtaining the quantity of water required to promote good health. Reliability may also influence quantity of water

collected. Intermittency of water supply, which is a common occurrence in most cities and towns, is an indication that reliability may influence quantity of water. Cost may also affect quantity of water, particularly in the poor rural communities and the poor urban suburbs.

Secondly, the water that is consumed by four out of 10 households or by 8 million or more Ghanaians is obtained from unprotected sources that are indicative of a substantial risk to health[8]. Thus, provision of potable and safe water in the country is inundated with problems relating to quantity and quality.

A major challenge facing the country is therefore the provision of ample quantity of water required for direct consumption, hygiene, laundry and bathing in the light of the sustained population growth which places severe constraints on water availability to achieve development goals.

Surface Water Availability

Estimates by the authors indicate that even if all the available water in the basins is utilised (i.e. 100% achievable level of use), the Volta System will experience water stress after 2025, whereas the South-Western System is currently encountering water stress conditions. The Coastal Basin is presently experiencing absolute water scarcity conditions.

However, 100% of the total water flow is seldom possible to mobilise, especially in hot and flat countries. Where topographical constraints make water storage difficult, or where a hot climate causes large losses of stored water due to evaporation, it may be difficult to raise the water mobilization level above 20 or 30%. Assuming 30% achievable level of use, the whole of Ghana is experiencing severe water scarcity conditions at the moment. The water scarcity condition worsens with continued population growth. The situation is much more acute in the coastal areas where water availability per capita is much lower compared to that in the other basins; water availability per capita of 121 cubic metres in 2000 declined to 108 in 2005 and it is expected to fall to 77 cubic metres by the end of the first quarter of this century. In fact, Coastal areas are presently experiencing absolute scarcity and the situation worsens as the population expands. The fastest growing region (Greater Accra) in the country is located in this basin. The population of this region expanded at the annual growth rate of 4.4 per cent between 1984 and 2000. It is therefore not surprising that water is rationed and the inhabitants are currently living through absolute water scarcity. The South-Western Basin will however encounter absolute scarcity in 2010.

Domestic Water Demand

The estimated levels of demand far exceed that of production except in Greater Accra Region where the demand is currently slightly below the production level. The demand levels are about twice as high as the production levels in Sekondi/Takoradi, Cape Coast, Kumasi, Sunyani, Tamale and Bolgatanga and nearly three times as high in Koforidua. Wa exhibits a more serious scenario where the demand exceeds production by nearly 10 times. The escalating population pressure on water resources is depicted by the projected estimates for the next decade (i.e. 2005-2015). The estimates indicate that unless production is substantially increased in the coming years, it is very unlikely that the projected water demand could be met during the projection period.

Nevertheless, for the purpose of strategic planning, an assessment of the actual water availability for domestic consumption in these urban areas was carried out. The quantity of water potentially available to serve the urban dwellers ranges from about 7 litres per capita per day in Bolgatanga to 40 litres in the Greater Accra Region. The decreasing quantity of water available for use by each person in a day between 2005 and 2015, reflecting various levels of water scarcity that is being experienced by the urban communities, is indicative of population pressure. Overall, the available data indicate that levels of demand far exceed that of supply. The huge gap between demand and supply therefore poses a big challenge towards the achievement of water related millennium development goals.

Groundwater has been found to be a reliable source of water both in terms of quantity and quality for the rural communities. The available information shows that the national coverage for potable water supply in the rural communities increased from 41% in 1984 to 52% in 1998 and declined to 44% in 2000. The fall in the national coverage for the rural areas is mostly attributable to population expansion.

To achieve 100% coverage of the rural population by 2015 will require a huge financial investment. Provision of adequate and clean drinking water for promotion of sustainable good health and reduction of deaths caused by water-borne and related diseases among the rural communities will require a great effort in terms of financial investment and technology to ensure access to, at least, basic level service in all rural areas by 2015.

Policy Implications

A major challenge facing the country is the provision of ample quantity of water required for direct consumption, hygiene, laundry and bathing in the light of the sustained population growth. Population expansion tends to engender severe water sustainability problems such as rapidly increasing water scarcity and protection of water quality in order to avoid the menace of water-related diseases.

Provision of basic level of access must be the highest priority for the water and health sectors. Hygiene cannot be assured and consumption requirements may be at risk. Concerted efforts should therefore be made to provide the increasing numbers of households with basic level of service. At this level of service, it is the effective use of the available water for hand and face-washing as well as household water treatment that controls infectious disease transmission. Interventions to promote good hygiene behaviours will augment health benefits and reduce health risks.

However, major improvements in health are achieved

by upgrading the basic level to the intermediate level for the increasing number of households. Furthermore, health and other benefits from improved water supply are significantly greater when there is a supply of continuous access to safe drinking water within the house. Upgrading of the service level improves household water security and contributes to the reduction of poverty.

Access to water sufficient for small-scale productive activity such as food production in the poor urban communities forms an important component of the poverty reduction strategy and may also generate significant indirect health benefits.

Studies consistently show that the use of water is important for controlling disease and that lack of access to water adversely affects health. Consequently, reaching the UN Millennium Development Goal to 'halve the proportion of people who are unable to reach or to afford safe drinking water by 2015' will require great effort on the part of all stakeholders.

Finally, the findings of this study indicate that demographic trends play a critical role in increasing demand for water. Policy-makers, decision-makers as well as water management specialists seriously need to understand and assess these trends and integrate them into the development programmes. Even in high-income countries, purely technical solutions mitigate only some of the demand for water. In the long term, slowing population growth and effectively implementing policies and programmes for improved water management are critical to sustainable development.

References

Community Water and Sanitation Agency, 2004. "Strategic Investment Plan 2000-2015" Ministry of Works and Housing, Accra .

Fakenmark, M. 1990. "Rapid Population growth and Water Scarcity: The Predicament of Tomorrow's Africa in Davis, K. and Berstein, M, S. (eds.), *Resources, Environment and Population: Present Knowledge and Future Options.* Population Council New York.

Fakenmark, M. 1989. "Macro-scale water scarcity requires micro- scale Approaches: Aspects of vulnerability in semi-arid development", *Natural Resources Forum 13 (4) 255-267.*

Gaisie, S. K. 2004. "Population Projections 2000-2025", Ghana Statistical Service, Accra.

Ghana Statistical Service (GSS), 1984. "1984 Population Census of Ghana", *The Gazetter 1&2* , GSS, Accra.

Ghana Statistical Service (GSS), 2005. "2000 Population and Housing Census of Ghana". The GSS, Accra.

Ghana Water Company, 2004. "List of Water supply Systems". Accra.

Gyau-Boakye, P. 2001. "Sources of Rural Water Supply in Ghana" in *International Water Resources Association,* vol.26, no.1, pp. 96-104.

Gyau-Boakye et al. 2002. "Management of Fresh Water Bodies in Ghana" in *International Water Resources Association,* vol.27,no.4, pp. 476-484.

Ministry of Works and Housing, 1998. "Ghana's Water Resources Management: Challenges and Opportunities". Accra.

APPENDIX

Appendix A.Table1. Households by Main Source of Drinking Water and Region [%]

Region	Pipe-Borne [inside]	Pipe-Borne [outside]	Tanker Supply	Well	Bore Hole	Spring/ Rain Water	River/Stream /Lake	Dug-out	Other
Western	8.5	23.2	0.7	23.2	14.2	2.7	24.1	1.5	0.2
Central	9.4	40.6	4.9	11.5	17.3	1.4	11	2.4	0.2
G/Accra	35.9	45	7.3	5.4	1.1	5.8	1.6	1.9	0.4
Volta	4.6	20.3	0.7	23	9.3	5.2	25.7	10.1	0.5
Eastern	8.8	19.4	0.6	23	16.4	3.7	23.6	2.9	0.1
Ashanti	19.3	20.7	0.6	15.6	22.5	5.5	14.1	1.3	0.3
B/Ahafo	5.1	18.4	0.7	12.6	25.3	4.4	26.2	3.1	0.1
Northern	7.6	14.8	0.9	31.6	17	10.7	22.8	19.6	0.3
Upper East	4.9	8.3	0.5	31.6	36.6	10.7	4.5	2.6	0.3
Upper West	4.5	11.1	0.6	10.6	47.8	1.31	7.6	4.5	0.2
All Regions	14.3	25.6	2.2	16.6	16.4	4.4	24.1	1.5	0.2

130

Appendix A Table 2. Population by Main Source of Drinking Water and Region, 2000 [%]

Region	Pipe-Borne	Tanker Supply	Well	Bore Hole	Spring/ Rain Water	River/Stream /Lake	Dug-out	Other	Total
Western	609900	14424	445409	272567	84022	463711	29525	4066	1923624
Central	804566	79398	184703	278119	43445	177294	38579	2556	1608660
G/Accra	2328810	210202	154197	30516	41469	45614	53328	14288	2878424
Volta	403923	11661	373580	150879	94324	417901	164289	8338	1624895
Eastern	592972	12949	481924	343523	108578	496368	60288	3138	2099785
Ashanti	1447653	24809	633138	814350	132246	510438	46539	7213	3616386
B/Ahafo	426995	12004	283089	459298	101151	475760	56403	1585	1816285
Northern	407777	17109	229259	308432	79150	414548	355548	5106	1816929
Upper East	121997	4960	291603	338509	98438	41197	24205	2982	923891
Upper West	90137	3708	61654	277128	76133	44194	26244	1037	580235
All Regions	7234730	391224	3138556	3273321	858956	3087025	854948	50354	1.888911E+7

131

Appendix B Table 1 Households by Access to Toilet Facility and Region [%]

Source	Western	Central	G/Accra	Volta	Eastern	Ashanti	B/Ahafo	Northern	U-East	U-West
Water Closet	7.2	4.9	22.1	2.5	4	11.6	3	2.5	2.5	2.5
Pit Latrine	30.4	25.1	11.2	28.6	37.5	20.5	31.8	1.9	1.5	2.5
KVIP	5.7	7	10.1	6.1	7	7.7	7.7	2.3	1.6	4.3
Bucket/Pan	2.7	2.8	9.1	4.8	5.5	2.8	1	1.6	1.4	1.9
Toilet Facility in another house	7.5	4.4	8.7	11.1	10.6	5.5	2.3	1	8.3	9.1
Public Toilet	34.2	37.6	27	21.9	29.8	46.3	39.7	14.5	6.3	10.1
No Facility	12.3	18.2	11.8	25	5.5	5.7	14.6	76.1	78.5	69.6
Total	100	100	100	100	100	100	100	100	100	100

Appendix B Table 2 Households by Access to Toilet Facility and Region Capitals [%]

Source	Takoradi	Cape Coast	/Accra	Ho	Koforidua	Kumasi	Sunyani	Tamale	Bolga	Wa
Water Closet	28.2	33.4	23.2	22.9	22.3	27.8	26.5	8.5	15.2	9
Pit Latrine	6.3	3.5	6.1	11.6	11.3	12	13.4	1.6	2.4	4.6
KVIP	4.8	5	11.7	9.1	6.4	9.3	7.2	6.3	2.7	8.4
Bucket/Pan	2.7	7.5	12.7	5.2	18.6	5.3	1.6	8.4	2.9	2.5
Toilet Facility in another house	5.9	2.6	9.3	7	3.2	5.6	1.5	1.8	4.5	8
Public Toilet	46	46.5	32.7	38.6	36.9	36.8	48.3	54	32.2	39.3
No Facility	6	1.5	4.1	5.4	1.1	2.9	1.5	19.3	39.8	28
Total	100	100	100	100	100	100	100	100	100	100

Chapter 6

HIV/AIDS and Survival Challenges in Sub-Saharan Africa: An Illustration with Ghana and South Africa

Chuks J. Mba

Introduction and Rationale

The acquired immune deficiency syndrome (AIDS), which is caused by the human immunodeficiency virus (HIV), emerged in the 1980s as the most terrifying epidemic of modern times. The AIDS pandemic affects primarily young to middle-aged adults, on whom both the national economy and family survival depend. HIV/AIDS has the potential to devastate human development, setting countries backward in their efforts to increase infant and child survival, achieve longer life expectancy and promote better life chances through education, as well as productive and secure livelihoods.

Worldwide, AIDS kills more than 8,000 people every day; one person every 10 seconds, while one child dies and one child is infected every minute. Out of a total of 39.4 million adults (defined as people aged 15-49) and children (defined as people below age 15) estimated to be living with HIV as of end of 2004, 25.4 million of them, representing about 64%, are from sub-Saharan Africa (UNAIDS/WHO 2005). Available evidence indicates that whereas 10.6 million adults lived with HIV/AIDS in 1994 in sub-Saharan Africa, there were about 30 million adults and children living with the disease by 2003, with 3.5 million new infections in 2002 alone (UNAIDS/WHO 2004; 2002). According to the estimates of UNAIDS (2002), the HIV prevalence rate in adults aged 15-49 ranges from 1.6 to 11.8% in Western Africa, from 0.1 to 2.6% in Northern Africa, from 3.6 to 12.9% in Central Africa, and from 2.8 to 15.0% in Southern Africa.

Of the 45 countries most severely affected by HIV/AIDS, 35 of them (78%) are in sub-Saharan Africa (United Nations, 2001)[9]. It is conceded that there are no simple explanations as to why some countries are more affected by HIV than others. However, poverty, illiteracy and engaging in identified risk behaviours account for much of the epidemic (Mba, 2003a; Caldwell, 2000; Mbamaonyeukwu, 2001a; 2000; Philipson and Posner, 1995). People who are infected with HIV often have no symptoms of disease for many years and can infect others without realising that they themselves are infected. The HIV continues to spread in Africa and around the world, moving into communities previously little troubled by the epidemic and strengthening its grip on areas where AIDS is already the leading cause of death in adults. Unless a cure is found, or life-prolonging therapy can be made more widely available, the majority of those now living with HIV will die within a decade.

Against this background, it is important to raise awareness and expanding knowledge about the deleterious effect of HIV/AIDS on Africa's life expectancy, with particular reference to South Africa and Ghana, for possible policy interventions. Apart from the fact that relevant data to warrant this study are available for the two countries, available evidence suggests that about 3.1% of the adult population in Ghana are living with the HIV virus, while the prevalence rate is about 21.5% in South Africa. Besides, South Africa has the highest number of HIV/AIDS persons in the world (6 million people; 600 die everyday). It should be noted also that many southern and eastern African countries had HIV prevalence rates in the late 1980s similar to those currently found in Ghana, but the situation worsened rapidly. This suggests that an unchecked epidemic could lead to much higher prevalence levels in Ghana. The two countries are therefore selected because they lie at opposite ends of the spectrum, so that analyzing their HIV/AIDS profiles will reveal more clearly the devastating impact of the pandemic.

Given these unsettling realities, it is important to find out what some of the severely affected countries are doing to combat the HIV/AIDS pandemic. In particular, the following key research questions are addressed in this study: What are the current HIV/AIDS prevalence levels across Africa? How far have we come with respect to combating HIV/AIDS? What is the contribution of HIV/AIDS mortality to the overall mortality of South Africa and Ghana? To what extent will life expectancy be enhanced if HIV/AIDS were absent in the mortality experience of these countries? What are the successes that have been chalked in the endeavour to combat HIV/AIDS? What lessons have been learnt? and what are the challenges being experienced by these countries?

In an attempt to answer these questions, this chapter first focuses on country-specific experiences with particular reference to national HIV prevalence levels, simulates what life expectancy will be in Ghana and South Africa with and without HIV/AIDS, examines responses and challenges, and then moves to a more holistic discussion of the HIV/AIDS situation on the African continent.

Data and Methods

The data for the present study are basically secondary. They emanate from three principal sources: the 1996 Census data file of South Africa, the report of the 2000 Population and Housing Census of Ghana (Ghana Statistical Service, 2002), and United Nations agencies, particularly the Joint United Nations Programme on HIV/AIDS and World Health Organization, as well as

World Population Prospects of the Population Division of the Department of Economic and Social Affairs of the United Nations. Additionally, use is made of documented research information resulting from data collected by key national institutions in the selected countries. The countries selected for specific mention in this paper are all in sub-Saharan Africa because, as pointed out previously, empirical evidence suggests that North Africa has the lowest HIV prevalence rate in Africa (UNAIDS/WHO 2005; United Nations 2001).

It is accepted that the statistics from these United Nations agencies are authentic. But little details are furnished concerning how the data were collected and methods used. As a result, measuring the quality and reliability of the data cannot be carried out (Mba, 2004a). Similar considerations underlie the use of data from various governmental and nongovernmental bodies reported in this study.

For purposes of comparison and ease of analysis, it would have been ideal to shift the 2000 Census results of Ghana to 1996 on the assumption of constant age structure since no significant changes occurred during the period 1996-2000 that would warrant major shifts in the demographic profile of Ghana[10]. However, due to paucity of reliable mortality data in Ghana, credible information on actual deaths by age group for 1996, critical for the analysis, was not available at the time of this study. As a result, the 2000 census figures are used in conjunction with Ghana's mortality profile for 2000 provided by the World Health Organization (2002).

The online version of the 1997-1999 World Health Statistics Annual (World Health Organization, 2001) contains all data that have been received by the world body since the publication of the 1996 edition. The available data are official national statistics since they have been transmitted to the World Health Organization by the appropriate and competent government agencies of the various countries, including South Africa Annual (World Health Organization, 2001). Unfortunately, the actual number of AIDS cases is not known because of underdiagnosis, incomplete reporting and reporting delays not only in South Africa and Ghana but also in other parts of Africa (World Health Organization, 2001; Dorrington et al., 2001; UNAIDS, 2000; UNAIDS/World Health Organization, 2000; Zimbabwe Ministry of Health, 1995). However, a technical report of the Medical Research Council of South Africa on the impact of HIV/AIDS estimated that AIDS deaths in South Africa accounted for about 14% of all deaths by 1996 (Dorrington et al., 2001). The present study employs this information on the assumption that it furnishes a credible evidence of the HIV/AIDS mortality experience of the South African society. Then, postulating that the age structure of the HIV/AIDS mortality provided by the World Health Organization (2001) is relevant, the proportion of deaths due to HIV/AIDS for each age group can then be estimated by applying the 14% to the age structure to the World Health statistics that specifies causes of death for various age groups for each country (World Health Organization, 2001). This principle is further used in the case of Ghana, on the assumption that the proportion of deaths due to AIDS at each age group is the same for both countries since Ghana's age distribution of AIDS mortality for 2000 is not available at the time of this study[11]. However, available evidence indicates that deaths due to AIDS constituted about 4.6% in 1994 and 9.4% in 1999 of the total number of deaths in Ghana (Ministry of Health, 2001). This implies that the proportion of deaths due to AIDS was about 10.4% of the total deaths in 2000[12].

It should be noted that the data provided by the World Health Organization (2001) from age 5 to age 74 are in broad 10-year age groups. Therefore, the Karup-King interpolation multipliers are employed to break them into 5-year age groups (Shryock and Siegel, 1976). Results of this computation are shown in the $_nD_x^i$ columns.

In an attempt to determine the effect of death due to HIV/AIDS on the overall mortality experience of South Africa and Ghana, the present study employs the multiple decrement life table techniques (Preston et al., 2000; Namboodiri and Suchindran, 1987; Keyfitz, 1985; Chiang, 1968). The multiple decrement procedures are based on the principle of competing risk; that is, as human beings are exposed to the risk of dying, death could result from various causes. The basic assumption underlying this principle is that the various causes of death are mutually exclusive and exhaustive (Preston et al., 2000; Namboodiri, 1991; Chiang, 1984). The assumption of independence implies that the force of the mortality function from different causes is additive. In the specific context of South Africa and Ghana, the state of interest is being alive and decrements from that state are attributable to HIV/AIDS and all other causes of death. Drawing from the conventional life table technique, the force of decrement from all causes combined is the sum of the force of decrement from HIV/AIDS and the force of decrement from all other causes. That is: $\mu(x) = \mu^1(x) + \mu^2(x) + \ldots + \mu^k(x)$.

Thus, the force of decrement from cause i at age x is simply the rate at which persons are leaving the defined state from cause i.

Because it is not possible in real life situations to observe directly associated single decrement processes, that is, processes in which one decrement alone is operating, certain functions defined for the basic life table can be extended to the associated single decrement life table. Associated with each decrement i in a multiple decrement process is a force of decrement function, $\mu^1(x)$. In general, the rate of decrement from $\mu^1(x)$ if i were the only decrement differs from what it would be if i were working in the presence of other decrements. The interest here is to determine the resultant life table, called the associated single decrement life table, if only the HIV/AIDS (i) of decrement were operating to reduce the populations of South Africa and Ghana. The decrement of interest is simply all decrements other than i (that is, - i). Thus, the task is to construct a table based on $\mu^{-i}(x)$ in which cause i will be arbitrarily deleted from the set of multiple decrements.

It should be stated that in the ensuing analysis, the estimation of life table functions, such as $_na_x$, $_nq_x$, $_nd_x$, $_nL_x$, and so on, follows the usual conventional approach. However, the calculation of the mean number of person-years lived in the interval by those dying in the interval, $_na_x$, is based on Chiang's (1968) approach for ages above age 4, while for children below age 5, the procedure suggested by Coale and Demeny (1983) is adopted. The probability of dying from the HIV/AIDS, $_nq_x^i$, is computed by applying the proportion of deaths that are due to the HIV/AIDS to the overall probability of dying between ages x and $x+n$, $_nq_x$, as indicated hereunder:

$$_nq_x^i = {_nq_x} \frac{_nD_x^i}{_nD_x}$$

where $_nD_x^i$ is the observed total number of deaths from HIV/AIDS between ages x and $x+n$, and $_nD_x$ is the observed total number of deaths from *all causes* between ages x and $x+n$.

In constructing the associated single decrement life table, the constant of proportionality for decrement other than HIV/AIDS in the interval x to $x+n$, R^{-i} is computed using the formula:

$$R^{-i} = \frac{_nD_x - {_nD_x^i}}{_nD_x}$$

Also, the probability of surviving from age x to age $x+n$ in the absence of HIV/AIDS, $_np_x^{-i}$, is estimated using the following formula proposed by Chiang (1968):

$$_np_x^{-i} = [_np_x]^{R^{-i}}$$

while the average person-years lived between ages x and $x+n$ in the absence HIV/AIDS, $_na_x^{-i}$, is calculated using the formula:

$$_na_x^{-i} = n + R^{-i} \frac{_nq_x}{_nq_x^{-i}} (_na_x - n)$$

for $x=0$, 1, 5 (ages under 10 years) and 70 (70-74 age group); but for the intervening age groups, ($x=10$ to 65), this formula is employed:

$$_5a_x^{-i} = \frac{-\dfrac{5}{24} {_5d_{x-5}^{-i}} + 2.5 {_5d_x^{-i}} + \dfrac{5}{24} {_5d_{x+5}^{-i}}}{_5d_x^{-i}}$$

However, it should be emphasized that vital registration system in South Africa and Ghana is not complete (Dorrington et al., 2001), implying that death registration coverage is not complete. Consequently, caution should be exercised while interpreting the results of subsequent analysis.

Current Prevalence Levels and Impact of HIV/AIDS

HIV Prevalence Levels and National Responses

Large variations exist between individual countries. The evidence presented in Table 1 shows that national HIV prevalence rates vary greatly between countries. In Somalia, Benin, and Senegal the prevalence is under 2% of the adult population, whereas in Malawi, Namibia, and Zambia around 20% of the adult population is infected.

In four Southern African countries, the national adult HIV prevalence rate has risen higher than was thought possible and now exceeds 24%. These countries, ranked in descending order, are Swaziland (38.8%), Botswana (37.3%), Lesotho (28.9%), and Zimbabwe (24.6%).

West Africa is relatively less affected by HIV infection, but the prevalence rates in some countries are creeping up. In West and Central Africa, HIV prevalence is estimated to exceed 5% in several countries including Cameroon (6.9%), Central African Republic (13.5%), Côte d'Ivoire (7.0%) and Nigeria (5.4%).

It should be noted that until recently the national prevalence rate has remained relatively low in Nigeria, the most populous country in Africa. The rate has grown slowly from 1.9% in 1993 to 5.4% in 2003 (UNAIDS 2005). But some states in Nigeria are already experiencing HIV prevalence rates as high as those now found in Cameroon. Table 1 indicates that already around 3.5 million Nigerians are estimated to be living with HIV, the next highest after South Africa (5.0 million).

HIV infection in Eastern Africa varies between adult prevalence rates of 4.9% in Democratic Republic of Congo to 16.5% in Zambia. In Uganda the countrywide prevalence among the adult population is 4.1%, which represents a success story from its previous high prevalence level (UNAIDS 2005).

As the total number of persons infected with HIV has been increasing across the African region (overwhelming majority of whom are adults aged 15-49), the number of HIV/AIDS orphans has also been on steady increase in much of Africa (UNAIDS/WHO 2005). While in some African countries, the epidemic is still growing despite its severity, others face a growing danger of explosive growth. The sharp rise in HIV prevalence among pregnant women in Cameroon (more than doubling to over 11% among those aged 20-24 between 1998 and 2000) shows how suddenly the epidemic can surge (UNAIDS, 2005).

A sizeable number of African countries now have five-year strategic plans designed to prevent and control HIV/AIDS (Economic Commission for Africa 2004). National AIDS Commissions have also been established in these countries which serve as advisory bodies to co-ordinate and oversee HIV/AIDS programmes for national responses. For example, the National AIDS Control Council was established in 1999 in Kenya, while the Ghana AIDS Commission and the National AIDS Commission were established in 2000 in Ghana and Liberia, respectively.

Also, many HIV/AIDS oriented policy documents have been developed and disseminated in many of these countries. These documents include HIV/AIDS/STIs Policies, and HIV/AIDS Strategic Frameworks for multi-sectoral responses. In Ethiopia, for instance, the Government adopted an HIV/AIDS policy in 1998. In recognition of the relevance of the HIV/AIDS pandemic to Africa's developmental aspirations, these documents call for multi-sectoral and multi-disciplinary response to confront and bring the pandemic under control. They provide broad guidelines for relevant sector Ministries, Departments, Agencies, Private sector, NGOs, and civil society to initiate specific programmes to address issues related to the risks and vulnerabilities of individuals and groups.

Table 1: Distribution of Countries in sub-Sahara Africa in decreasing order according to the HIV Prevalence Rates.

Country	Rank	Adult rate (%)	Total number of persons infected	Number of adults infected (15-49)	Number of Orphans
Swaziland	1	38.8	170,000	150,000	35,000
Botswana	2	37.3	330,000	300,000	69,000
Lesotho	3	28.9	360,000	330,000	73,000
Zimbabwe	4	24.6	2,300,000	2,000,000	780,000
Namibia	5	22.5	230,000	200,000	47,000
South Africa	6	21.5	5,000,000	4,700,000	660,000
Zambia	7	16.5	1,200,000	1,000,000	570,000
Malawi	8	14.2	850,000	780,000	470,000
CAR	9	13.5	250,000	220,000	110,000
Mozambique	10	12.2	1,100,000	1,000,000	420,000
Tanzania	11	8.8	1,500,000	1,300,000	810,000
Cote d'Ivoire	12	7.0	770,000	690,000	420,000
Cameroon	13	6.9	920,000	860,000	210,000
Kenya	14	6.7	2,500,000	2,300,000	890,000
Burundi	15	6.0	390,000	330,000	240,000
Nigeria	16	5.4	3,500,000	3,200,000	1,000,000
Rwanda	17	5.1	500,000	430,000	260,000
Ethiopia	18	4.4	2,100,000	1,900,000	990,000
DR Congo	19	4.2	1,300,000	1,100,000	930,000
Uganda	20	4.1	600,000	510,000	880,000
Togo	21	4.1	150,000	110,000	63,000
Ghana	22	3.1	350,000		
Benin	23	1.9	120,000	110,000	34,000
Somalia	24	1.0	43,000	43,000	
Senegal	25	0.8	27,000	24,000	15,000

Source: UNAIDS, 2005. 2004 Report on the Global AIDS Epidemic.

Furthermore, UNAIDS country offices throughout the region focus on empowering leadership, building partnerships and mobilizing resources for effective national responses. The UNAIDS is also helping countries to strengthen their management and utilization of strategic information; and to build capacities for tracking, monitoring and evaluating national responses to AIDS.

A continuing rise in the number of HIV infected people is not inevitable. There is growing evidence that prevention efforts can be effective, and this includes initiatives in some of the most heavily affected countries (UNAIDS/WHO 2005; Bennell et al., 2002; Arthur et al., 2000; Miller and Yaeger, 1995). In some countries there have been early and sustained prevention efforts. For example in Senegal there was effective prevention, which is still reflected in the relatively low adult prevalence rate. Also, Uganda shows that a widespread epidemic can be brought under control. Few localised studies in Zambia have also shown success in prevention efforts. These prevention efforts include less sexual activity, having fewer multiple partners, and more consistent use of condoms. Awareness campaigns and prevention programmes in South Africa are now starting to work.

Life Table Analysis of Ghana and South Africa
Tables 2a and 2b show the multiple decrement life tables of South Africa in 1996 and Ghana in 2000 constructed with a view to finding out the contribution of HIV/AIDS to the overall mortality experience of the two countries. The findings reveal that the infant mortality rate and under five mortality rate are respectively about 23 deaths per 1,000 live births, and 25 deaths per 1,000 live births in case of South Africa, and 98 deaths per 1,000 live births and 105 deaths per 1,000 live births, respectively for Ghana. The mortality estimates translate into expectations of life at birth of 63.6 years for South Africa and 53.3 years for Ghana. These findings are consistent with mortality estimates for both countries from other sources (World Health Organization , 2002; Ghana Statistical Service, 2002; United Nations, 2001a; Udjo, 2001; World Bank, 2000; Ghana Statistical Service and Macro International, 1999; Republic of South Africa, 1997; Kinsella and Ferreira, 1997).

Tables 2a and 2b further show that the proportion of new born babies that will eventually die from HIV/AIDS under the South Africa's age-cause-specific death rates of 1996 is 5.7%, while the corresponding figure for Ghana under the age-cause-specific death rates of 2000 is 7.2%. Furthermore, 7.7% and 11.5% of South Africans who survive to age 60 years, and 75 years and above, respectively will die of HIV/AIDS under the prevailing age-specific mortality conditions[13]. The corresponding figures for Ghana are respectively 13.0% and 23.4%. The results seem to suggest that under the prevailing mortality conditions, more Ghanaians than South Africans are likely to die of AIDS even though the HIV/AIDS prevalence rate is significantly lower in Ghana[14].

Tables 3a and 3b indicate the associated single decrement life table for South Africa and Ghana, respectively under a hypothetical scenario whereby HIV/AIDS is deleted to determine the extent of the resultant gain in expectation of life in the two countries. The findings depicted in Table 3a show that, for South Africa, the probability of surviving to age 75 in the absence of HIV/AIDS is 0.53 (53454/100000), which is higher than 0.48 (48471/100000), the probability of surviving to age 75 for all causes combined. This translates into a gain in life expectancy at birth of 26 years, from 63.6 years for all causes combined to 89.8 years in the absence of HIV/AIDS. Table 2b suggests that for Ghana, the probability of surviving to age 75 in the absence of HIV/AIDS is 0.34, which is higher than 0.31, the probability of surviving to age 75 for all causes combined. This translates into a gain in life expectancy at birth of about 10 years, from 53.3 years for all causes combined to 63.0 years in the absence of HIV/AIDS. These results show that there is a significant improvement in the mortality profile of each country less HIV/AIDS disease.

This tremendous gain in both the number of persons surviving to each age and expectation of life is better illustrated pictorially in Figures 1a and b. The graphs indicate that there is a pronounced gain in life expectancy at every age with the deletion of HIV/AIDS.

Due to better healthcare and public health measures, as well as improved nutritional and sanitary conditions, South Africa's mortality profile is better than that of Ghana. The results of this analysis support this contention. In general, though, the findings indicate that South Africa's life expectancy will fare tremendously better if the HIV/AIDS scourge is eliminated or drastically reduced.

Table 2a. Multiple Decrement Life Table of South Africa, 1996

Age x	$_nN_x$	$_nD_x$	$_nm_x$	$_na_x$	$_nq_x$	$_np_x$	l_x	$_nd_x$	$_nL_x$	T_x	e^0_x	$_nD_x$	$_nq^i_x$	$_nd^i_x$	l^i_x	$_nm^i_x$
0	856239	20045	0.0234	0.113	0.0229	0.9771	100000	2293	97966	6356769	63.6	3585	0.0041	410	5660	0.0042
1	3587382	6431	0.0018	1.583	0.0071	0.9929	97707	698	389140	6258802	64.1	1374	0.0015	149	5655	0.0004
5	4668722	1822	0.0004	2.233	0.0019	0.9981	97009	189	484522	5869663	60.5	34	0.0000	4	5650	0.0000
10	4654100	2543	0.0005	2.309	0.0027	0.9973	96820	264	483389	5385141	55.6	67	0.0001	7	5645	0.0000
15	4180716	6484	0.0016	2.430	0.0077	0.9923	96556	746	480862	4901752	50.8	1307	0.0016	150	5640	0.0003
20	3982353	9116	0.0023	2.450	0.0114	0.9886	95810	1090	476270	4420890	46.1	2848	0.0036	341	5635	0.0007
25	3455728	12058	0.0035	2.463	0.0173	0.9827	94720	1638	469443	3944621	41.6	5896	0.0085	801	5630	0.0017
30	3074201	13368	0.0043	2.467	0.0215	0.9785	93082	2002	460338	3475178	37.3	6332	0.0102	948	5625	0.0021
35	2653755	12857	0.0048	2.469	0.0239	0.9761	91080	2180	449882	3014839	33.1	4389	0.0082	744	5620	0.0017
40	2138626	13211	0.0062	2.470	0.0304	0.9696	88900	2704	437663	2564957	28.9	3250	0.0075	665	5615	0.0015
45	1677525	13739	0.0082	2.470	0.0401	0.9599	86197	3458	422236	2127294	24.7	1977	0.0058	498	5610	0.0012
50	1268895	14705	0.0116	2.467	0.0563	0.9437	82739	4657	401895	1705059	20.6	1139	0.0044	361	5605	0.0009
55	1069936	15682	0.0147	2.462	0.0707	0.9293	78081	5517	376406	1303163	16.7	670	0.0030	236	5600	0.0006
60	890536	16675	0.0187	2.455	0.0894	0.9106	72564	6485	346320	926757	12.8	302	0.0016	117	5595	0.0003
65	758887	17345	0.0229	2.448	0.1080	0.8920	66079	7135	312187	580437	8.8	168	0.0010	69	5590	0.0002
70	482163	18866	0.0391	2.416	0.1777	0.8223	58944	10473	267658	268250	4.6	34	0.0003	19	5585	0.0001
75	1183808	44531	0.0376	0.012	1.0000	0.0000	48471	48471	592	592	0.0	130	0.0029	142	5580	0.0001

Sources: South Africa's 1996 Census (for $_nN_x$ values) and World Health Organization, 2001 (for $_nD_x$ values).

Note: $_nN_x$ =Population size between ages x and x+n; $_nD_x$ =Total number of deaths between ages x and x+n; $_nm_x$ =Observed age-specific death rates between ages x and x+n; $_na_x$ = Average person-years lived between ages x and x+n; $_nq_x$ = Probability of dying between ages x and x+n; $_np_x$ = Probability of surviving from age x to age x+n; l_x =Number of people left alive at age x; $_nd_x$ =Number of people dying between ages x and x+n; $_nL_x$ = Person-years lived between ages x and x+n; T_x = Person-years lived above age x; e^0_x=Life Expectancy at age x; $_nD^i_x$ =Total number of deaths from HIV/AIDS between ages x and x+n; $_nq^i_x$ = Probability of dying from HIV/AIDS between ages x and x+n; $_nd^i_x$ = Number of people dying from HIV/AIDS between ages x and x+n; l^i_x = Number of people left alive from HIV/AIDS at age x; $_nm^i_x$ = Observed age-specific death rates from HIV/AIDS between ages x and x+n.

Table 2b. Multiple Decrement Life Table of Ghana, 2000

Age x	$_nN_x$	$_nD_x$	$_nm_x$	$_na_x$	$_nq_x$	$_np_x$	l_x	$_nd_x$	$_nL_x$	T_x	e_x^0	$_nD_x^i$	$_nq_x^i$	$_nd_x^i$	l_x^i	$_nm_x^i$
0	525258	51209	0.0975	0.113	0.0897	0.9103	100000	8973	92042	5333435	53.3	2314	0.0041	405	7247	0.0044
1	2244163	16384	0.0073	1.583	0.0287	0.9713	91027	2612	357792	5241393	57.6	887	0.0016	141	7242	0.0004
5	2775206	4634	0.0017	2.434	0.0083	0.9917	88414	735	440186	4883601	55.2	22	0.0000	3	7237	0.0000
10	2262216	3009	0.0013	2.419	0.0066	0.9934	87679	581	436897	4443415	50.7	43	0.0001	8	7232	0.0000
15	1883753	4948	0.0026	2.455	0.0130	0.9870	87098	1136	432599	4006518	46.0	843	0.0022	194	7227	0.0004
20	1600820	7948	0.0050	2.469	0.0245	0.9755	85962	2108	424475	3573918	41.6	1838	0.0057	487	7222	0.0011
25	1487299	10614	0.0071	2.471	0.0350	0.9650	83854	2939	411838	3149443	37.6	3806	0.0126	1054	7217	0.0026
30	1206809	11159	0.0092	2.470	0.0452	0.9548	80915	3655	395327	2737605	33.8	4087	0.0165	1339	7212	0.0034
35	1029765	9946	0.0097	2.469	0.0471	0.9529	77260	3642	377082	2342278	30.3	2833	0.0134	1037	7207	0.0028
40	886931	8703	0.0098	2.469	0.0479	0.9521	73618	3524	359169	1965196	26.7	2097	0.0115	849	7202	0.0024
45	720357	7975	0.0111	2.468	0.0538	0.9462	70094	3774	340910	1606027	22.9	1276	0.0086	604	7197	0.0018
50	568369	7976	0.0140	2.463	0.0678	0.9322	66319	4493	320199	1265117	19.1	735	0.0062	414	7192	0.0013
55	355842	8177	0.0230	2.448	0.1085	0.8915	61826	6710	292003	944918	15.3	432	0.0057	354	7187	0.0012
60	366351	9415	0.0257	2.442	0.1206	0.8794	55116	6645	258584	652915	11.8	195	0.0025	138	7182	0.0005
65	258709	10559	0.0408	2.412	0.1846	0.8154	48470	8947	219203	394331	8.1	108	0.0019	92	7177	0.0004
70	225158	11420	0.0507	2.392	0.2240	0.7760	39524	8852	174536	175128	4.4	22	0.0004	17	7172	0.0001
75	515073	23768	0.0461	0.012	1.0000	0.0000	30671	30671	375	592	0.0	85	0.0036	110	7167	0.0002

Sources: Ghana's 2000 Census (for $_nN_x$ values) and World Health Organization, 2002 (for $_nD_x$ values).
Note: See Table 2a for explanation of the symbols.

Table 3a. Associated Single Decrement Life Table for Causes of Death other than HIV/AIDS, South Africa, 1996.

Age x	R^{-i}	l_x	$_np_x$	$_na_x$	$_nq_x$	e^o_x	$_np^{-i}_x$	$_nq^{-i}_x$	l^{-i}_x	$_na^{-i}_x$	$_nd^{-i}_x$	$_nm^{-i}_x$	$_nL^{-i}_x$	T^{-i}_x	e^{-i}_x
0	0.9620	100000	0.9771	0.113	0.0229	63.6	0.9779	0.0221	100000	0.114	2207	0.0225	98043	8975786	89.8
1	0.7792	97707	0.9929	1.583	0.0071	64.1	0.9944	0.0056	97793	1.585	544	0.0014	389855	8877742	90.8
5	0.4473	97009	0.9981	2.233	0.0019	60.5	0.9991	0.0009	97248	2.235	85	0.0002	486006	8487887	87.3
10	0.4833	96820	0.9973	2.309	0.0027	55.6	0.9987	0.0013	97163	2.751	128	0.0003	485528	8001880	82.4
15	0.3189	96556	0.9923	2.430	0.0077	50.8	0.9975	0.0025	97035	2.737	240	0.0005	484634	7516352	77.5
20	0.3652	95810	0.9886	2.450	0.0114	46.1	0.9958	0.0042	96795	2.754	404	0.0008	483071	7031718	72.6
25	0.4407	94720	0.9827	2.463	0.0173	41.6	0.9923	0.0077	96392	2.680	738	0.0015	480246	6548648	67.9
30	0.5099	93082	0.9785	2.467	0.0215	37.3	0.9890	0.0110	95654	2.630	1055	0.0022	475768	6068401	63.4
35	0.6227	91080	0.9761	2.469	0.0239	33.1	0.9850	0.0150	94599	2.639	1416	0.0030	469651	5592633	59.1
40	0.7118	88900	0.9696	2.470	0.0304	28.9	0.9783	0.0217	93183	2.649	2026	0.0044	461152	5122982	55.0
45	0.7919	86197	0.9599	2.470	0.0401	24.7	0.9681	0.0319	91157	2.657	2908	0.0065	448972	4661830	51.1
50	0.8576	82739	0.9437	2.467	0.0563	20.6	0.9515	0.0485	88249	2.617	4278	0.0099	431051	4212858	47.7
55	0.9052	78081	0.9293	2.462	0.0707	16.7	0.9358	0.0642	83971	2.587	5389	0.0133	406847	3781807	45.0
60	0.9368	72564	0.9106	2.455	0.0894	12.8	0.9160	0.0840	78581	2.561	6598	0.0175	376817	3374960	42.9
65	0.9508	66079	0.8920	2.448	0.1080	8.8	0.8971	0.1029	71984	2.624	7411	0.0217	342313	2998143	41.7
70	0.9661	58944	0.8223	2.416	0.1777	4.6	0.8278	0.1722	64573	2.424	11119	0.0378	294223	2655830	41.1
75	0.9814	48471	0.0000	0.012	1.0000	0.0	0.0000	1.0000	53454	0.012	53454	0.0369	2361606	2361606	44.2

Sources: South Africa's 1996 Census (for $_nN_x$ values) and World Health Organization, 2001 (for $_nD_x$ values).

Note: R^{-i} =Constant of proportionality for decrement other than HIV/AIDS in the interval x to x+n; l_x =Number of people left alive at age x; $_np_x$ = Probability of surviving from age x to age x+n; $_na_x$ = Average person-years lived between ages x and x+n; $_nq_x$ = Probability of dying between ages x and x+n; e^o_x =Life Expectancy at age x; $_np^{-i}_x$ = Probability of surviving from age x to age x+n in the absence of HIV/AIDS; $_nq^{-i}_x$ = Probability of dying between ages x and x+ndeaths between ages x and x+n in the absence of HIV/AIDS; l^{-i}_x =Number of people left alive at age x in the absence of HIV/AIDS; $_na^{-i}_x$ = Average person-years lived between ages x and x+n in the absence of HIV/AIDS; $_nd^{-i}_x$ = Number of people dying between ages x and x+n in the absence of HIV/AIDS; $_nm^{-i}_x$ =Observed age-specific death rates between ages x and x+n in the absence of HIV/AIDS; $_nL^{-i}_x$ = Person-years lived between ages x and x+n in the absence of HIV/AIDS; T^{-i}_x = Person-years lived above age x in the absence of HIV/AIDS; e^{-i}_x = Life Expectancy at age x in the absence of HIV/AIDS.

149

Table 3b. Associated Single Decrement Life Table for Causes of Death other than HIV/AIDS, Ghana, 2000.

Age x	R^i	l_x	$_np_x$	$_na_x$	$_nq_x$	e^o_x	$_np^i_x$	$_nq^i_x$	l^i_x	$_na^i_x$	$_nd^i_x$	$_nm^i_x$	$_nL^i_x$	T^i_x	e^i_x
0	0.9932	100000	0.9103	0.113	0.0897	53.3	0.9142	0.0858	100000	0.115	8583	0.0931	92400	6298441	63.0
1	0.9591	91027	0.9713	1.583	0.0287	57.6	0.9728	0.0272	91417	1.585	2484	0.0069	359672	6206041	67.9
5	0.8973	88414	0.9917	2.434	0.0083	55.2	0.9917	0.0083	88934	2.430	735	0.0017	442781	5846369	65.7
10	0.7989	87679	0.9934	2.419	0.0066	50.7	0.9935	0.0065	88199	2.577	574	0.0013	439605	5403588	61.3
15	0.5849	87098	0.9870	2.455	0.0130	46.0	0.9892	0.0108	87625	2.733	946	0.0022	435982	4963983	56.7
20	0.6599	85962	0.9755	2.469	0.0245	41.6	0.9811	0.0189	86679	2.622	1637	0.0038	429504	4528000	52.2
25	0.7046	83854	0.9650	2.471	0.0350	37.6	0.9774	0.0226	85042	2.578	1921	0.0046	420558	4098497	48.2
30	0.7268	80915	0.9548	2.47	0.0452	33.8	0.9711	0.0289	83121	2.565	2401	0.0059	409756	3677939	44.2
35	0.7739	77260	0.9529	2.469	0.0471	30.3	0.9661	0.0339	80720	2.528	2738	0.0069	396831	3268183	40.5
40	0.7963	73618	0.9521	2.469	0.0479	26.7	0.9634	0.0366	77982	2.543	2852	0.0074	382904	2871353	36.8
45	0.8346	70094	0.9462	2.468	0.0538	22.9	0.9546	0.0454	75130	2.592	3410	0.0093	367437	2488449	33.1
50	0.8780	66319	0.9322	2.463	0.0678	19.1	0.9383	0.0617	71720	2.662	4429	0.0127	348246	2121011	29.6
55	0.9154	61826	0.8915	2.448	0.1085	15.3	0.8969	0.1031	67291	2.579	6936	0.0218	319665	1772765	26.3
60	0.9472	55116	0.8794	2.442	0.1206	11.8	0.8817	0.1183	60355	2.580	7137	0.0252	284501	1453100	24.1
65	0.9632	48470	0.8154	2.412	0.1846	8.1	0.8171	0.1829	53218	2.555	9733	0.0404	242286	1168600	22.0
70	0.9735	39524	0.7760	2.392	0.2240	4.4	0.7764	0.2236	43484	2.393	9724	0.0506	192070	926313	21.3
75	0.9836	30671	0.0000	0.012	1.0000	0.0	0.0000	1.0000	33760	0.000	33760	0.0460	734243	734243	21.7

150

Sources: Ghana's 2000 Census (for $_nN_x$ values) and World Health Organization, 2002 (for $_nD_x$ values).
Note: See Table 3a for explanation of the symbols.

Figure 1a: Life Expectancy at Age x, 1996 (South Africa)

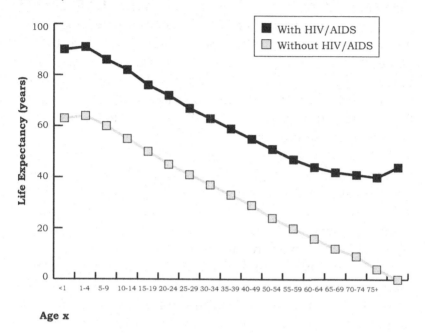

Figure 1b: Life Expectancy at Age x, 2000 (Ghana)

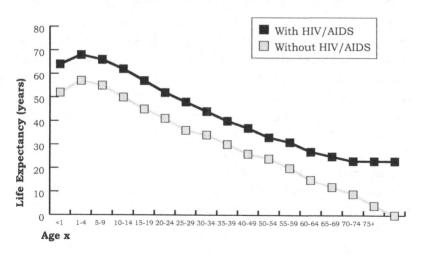

HIV/AIDS and Survival Challenges in Sub-Saharan Africa

Lessons Learnt and Challenges

Development partners such as the WHO, UNFPA, and UNICEF have contributed in influencing African governments, the general public, and civil society groups to place HIV/AIDS as a major developmental issue that requires urgent attention. As a result, religious, traditional, and community leaders, who are key to successful implementation of HIV/AIDS interventions, are supportive of these efforts.

Unfortunately, the high level of HIV/AIDS awareness among the general public has not translated into significant positive behavioural change. The lack of change in behaviour continues to produce a large pool of persons living with HIV/AIDS and to increase the burden of care, particularly for orphans and the aged.

There are weak institutional co-ordinating mechanisms and inadequate capacity to undertake HIV/AIDS activities at national and subnational levels in many of these countries. There is therefore the need for stronger institutional mechanisms to improve co-ordination of HIV/AIDS activities and community based initiatives.

The war situation in parts of Africa has not only aggravated poverty, but has led to more prostitution and unprecedented increase in the number of cases of sexual violence against women and girls, heightening the risk of HIV/AIDS transmission. Gender-based violence on the continent results in faster spread of the disease (Economic Commission for Africa, 2004). Tanzania, for example, is home to thousands of refugees from Burundi, Rwanda, and Democratic Republic of Congo. These refugees intermingle with Tanzanians and there are no existing HIV/AIDS programmes to cater for them. Besides, socio-cultural practices, attitudes, and beliefs hamper progress and accentuate stigma, denial, and discrimination against women and HIV/AIDS sufferers.

Gender is a cross-cutting issue and an important factor in the transmission of HIV/AIDS. Gender perspectives should be mainstreamed in HIV/AIDS country programmes. Specific messages on HIV prevention should be developed and target women, especially those attending ante-natal care clinics, while male involvement in reproductive health matters should not be relegated to the background. There should therefore be strong political commitment and openness at all levels – national, regional, district, local, and community – to fight the disease.

The overriding challenge facing the region in 2005 and beyond will be to translate promises and planned commitments into expanded services that rapidly reach the people who urgently need them. The resources and money available will need to be made to work in the most effective ways possible, in order to prevent new infections, provide treatment and support for people living with HIV, and to offer care and support to vulnerable sectors of society, such as orphans and the elderly. This will involve dynamic leadership and management to unlock the existing constraints on resource flows. It will also involve redoubled efforts to mobilize even more resources and close the existing funding gap.

For UNAIDS, the major challenge will be to deliver on the vision of scaling up country responses in an efficient and coordinated way. This will involve unblocking constraints (through better procurement, tendering, staff costs, simplification of procedures, etc) to available funding, and strengthening governance and management of national responses through better integration of global and country-level initiatives. This can be achieved by, *inter alia,* mainstreaming AIDS work into all sectors and development action.

Discussion

AIDS now represents the fourth most important cause of death worldwide and the leading cause in sub-Saharan Africa, the region most severely affected with about 70% of all infected persons. Within sub-Saharan Africa, the seven most affected countries are Botswana, Lesotho, Namibia, South Africa, Swaziland, Zambia, and Zimbabwe. Some probable reasons why the region has been particularly hard hit by the epidemic have been discussed elsewhere (Mba, 2003a; Mbamaonyeukwu, 2001a; Caldwell, 2000; Philipson and Posner, 1995).

The impact of HIV/AIDS on life expectancies, and on infant and child survival in the most affected countries is unmistakable. In Botswana and Zimbabwe, for example, the current life expectancy at birth is already below 40 years and is expected to fall during the 2010-2015 period to 31.6 and 33.0 years, respectively (United Nations, 2003). These extremely low values put these two and other severely affected countries back to levels of life expectancy prevalent before World War II or even in some cases at the beginning of the twentieth century. Botswana, which had one of the lowest child mortality rates in sub-Saharan Africa, saw its success eroded by the epidemic as mortality rates rose from 63 deaths per 1,000 live births in 1990-1995 to an estimated 104 deaths per thousand during the period 2000-2005 (United Nations, 2003).

There is one fundamental reason why HIV/AIDS is responsible for global divergence or a slowdown in convergence in levels of life expectancy. The highest HIV/AIDS prevalence rates are found in African countries, which are essentially countries faced with widespread poverty, low income levels, and deficient health care systems (Mba, 2003a; 2003b). This implies higher mortality than would result if economically and socially developed countries experienced similar HIV/AIDS prevalence rates.

Future trends in HIV/AIDS prevention efforts, in access to antiretroviral treatment, and in access to medical care more generally will have substantial effects on the future trend in life expectancies and infant and child survival rates in the affected countries. One would hope that greater and more equal access to medical care and treatment, more successful preventive measures, and perhaps even the discovery of a vaccine will mitigate the loss in human life caused by HIV/AIDS.

Nearly six million people in African and other developing countries have HIV infections that urgently require antiretroviral treatment to keep them alive and healthy (UNAIDS/WHO 2005). In 2002, WHO and UNAIDS launched the '3 by 5 initiative' which aims to offer anti-retroviral treatment to three million persons by the end of 2005. As of December 2004, an estimated 700,000 (630,000 to 780,000) persons were receiving antiretroviral treatment with an increase from 440,000 to 700,000 persons treated within the second half of 2004. The WHO (2004) Report shows how the history of HIV/AIDS has changed. It describes how innovative HIV/AIDS treatment programmes can save millions of lives in developing countries and how, crucially, such efforts can drive improvements in health systems. Unfortunately, to date, evidence about the success of HIV/AIDS treatment is available mostly from industrialized countries and more recently from Brazil, Thailand and some sites in Africa. In Africa, a tremendous scale-up is required to close the treatment gap.

As the implications of the global spread of AIDS have been more sharply perceived, it has also become increasingly apparent that AIDS is a social, economic, and political issue, just as much as a medical and demographic one. Since AIDS has no respect for national boundaries, the consequences of AIDS already have become a special concern for virtually all developing countries. We face the grim and sobering prospect that in many of these countries, based on the current HIV infection levels, the death rates from AIDS could equal or exceed the number of deaths from all other causes.

Furthermore, excluding the increasing number of children who succumb to AIDS, the persons who die of the disease are generally in the 15-49 age group, depriving countries already desperately lacking in human resources, of their most productive and reproductive citizens. In all likelihood, this group includes many of those who have the most to contribute to their countries' development. Additionally, there is the enormous cost of health care for governments, which today face extraordinary health constraints. These costs include not only the provision of direct hospital care to AIDS victims, but also the related costs of counselling, blood screening, medical supplies and training. Taken together, these costs can be expected to exceed by far other health expenditures, resulting in an enormous drain on resources. On top of the diversion of human and financial resources as a direct result of the HIV/AIDS, some of these countries will face indirect economic costs as a result of the lost years of production.

AIDS has a number of demographic and related consequences. Among the most important is the erosion of the support mechanisms of the elderly persons (Mba, 2004b; Mbamaonyeukwu, 2001b). Also, it has deleterious effects on future population growth, demand for health services, the size of the potential labour force, and educational needs (Takyi and Mba, 2005). Moreover, household composition and living arrangements are influenced by the AIDS pandemic through orphanhood and widowhood.

Given our traditional extended family system, there should be a strong interest in focusing on family as a strategy for HIV/AIDS prevention, care, and treatment in Africa. Research should examine home based care, particularly the role of caregivers (notably women) in the household. It is important to find out the role of the woman and her culture in care and support of a family member living with HIV/AIDS. For example, it is important to ascertain how women would normally care for the sick family members and what are some cultural resources that either prove to be supportive or problematic in their efforts.

One of the vexing issues in the debate between those who provide the resources (Western countries and United Nations agencies) and intellectuals and public health workers in African countries that receive these resources relates to basing HIV prevalence rates on estimates from projections based on women who visit antenatal clinics. It is not clear to what extent these samples represent the HIV prevalence rates in these countries.

David Gisselquist and colleagues (2003) contend that the Western fixation on African sexuality is one of the reasons it overlooks other roots of HIV transmissions notably use of injection in the hospitals and clinics. In fact, the authors report that their meta-analysis of the published work on HIV/AIDS in Africa lead them to conclude that "general population studies through 1988 suggest that medical exposures were responsible for more African HIV than sexual exposures" (Gisselquist et al. 2003: 151). The point here is not to endorse or reject this conclusion in terms of the proportion of the HIV transmitted in the clinic (it is generally agreed that some of the transmissions do occur in the clinics) but to question the politics of science that normalized sexuality as the only transmission route worthy of research investigation while ignoring other routes of transmission.

Adolescents have been identified as being at elevated risk for HIV infection (Mba, 2003a; Aggleton, 1995). Since the AIDS epidemic has had a disproportionate impact on the developing world, African adolescents may be at even higher risk than other teenagers from the rest of developing countries. "Sub-Saharan Africa remains by far the region worst-affected by the AIDS epidemic. The region has just over 10% of the world's population, but is home to two-thirds of all people living with HIV" (UNAIDS, 2005: 1). It is strongly advocated that sex educators in institutions of learning should now stress abstinence as the best way to avoid HIV/AIDS and pregnancy among unmarried teenagers. In a clear and unambiguous support of this fact, the Acting Governor of New Jersey, Donald T. Di-Francesco, signed bill that orders teachers of sex education to list abstinence as the only certain method to prevent pregnancy and sexually transmitted diseases, including HIV/AIDS (Associated Press, 2002).

Consequently, it can be contended that the HIV/AIDS pandemic demands an increased focus on prevention through increased public education while initiating efforts to engage in social transformation of contextual forces that promote vulnerability. Such a critical yet important approach demands a multisectoral response that is anchored in a multidisciplinary framing of research questions and understanding of the complexities of HIV/AIDS and how to successfully combat it.

References

Aggleton, P. 1995. Young People and AIDS. *AIDS Care,* Vol. 7. No. 1, pp.77-80.

Arthur, G., Bhatt, S, and Gilks, C. 2000. "The Impact of HIV/AIDS on Hospital Services in Developing Countries", *AIDS Analysis Africa,* Vol. 10, No. 6, pp.15-16.

Associated Press, 2002. "Teachers Must Stress Abstinence in Sex Education", cited in *Philadelphia METRO,* Thursday, January 3, 2002, p.05.

Bennell, P., Hyde, K., and Swainson, N. 2002. *The Impact of the HIV/AIDS Epidemic on the Education Sector in Sub-Saharan Africa: A Synthesis of the Findings and Recommendations of Three Country Studies.* Sussex: Centre for International Education, University of Sussex Institute of Education.

Caldwell, J.C. 2000. "Rethinking the African AIDS Epidemic", *Population and Development Review* Vol. 26, No. 1, pp. 117-135.

Chiang, C.L. 1984. *The Life Table and Its Applications.* Robert E. Krieger Publishing Company, Malabar, Florida.

Chiang, C.L. 1968. *Introduction to Stochastic Processes in Biostatistics.* Wiley Publishers, New York.

Coale, A. and Demeny, P. 1983. *Regional Model Life Tables and Stable Populations.* Academic Press, New York.

Dorrington, R., Bourne, D., Bradshaw, D., Laubscher, R. and Timaeus, I., 2001. *The Impact of HIV/AIDS on Adult Mortality in South Africa.* Technical Report, Burden of Disease Research Unit, Medical Research Council, South Africa.

Economic Commission for Africa (ECA) 2004. *ICPD 10th Anniversary: Africa Regional Review Report.* The ECA Addis Ababa. ECA/SDD/CM.ICPD at 10/2.

Ghana Statistical Service, 2002. *2000 Population and Housing Census: Summary Report of Final Results.* Ghana Statistical Service, Accra.

158

Gisselquist, D., Potterat, J.J., Brody, S. and Vachon, F. 2003. "Let it be Sexual: How Health Care Transmission of AIDS in Africa was Ignored", in *International Journal of STD & AIDS,* Vol. 14, pp.148-161.

Keyfitz, N. 1985. *Applied Mathematical Demography.* Springer Texts in Statistics, Springer-Verlag, New York.

Mba, C.J. 2004a. "Challenges of Population Census Enumeration in Africa: An Illustration with the Age-Sex Data of The Gambia", in *Research Review,* Vol. 20, No. 1, pp.9-19.

Mba, C.J. 2004b. "Population Ageing and Survival Challenges in Rural Ghana" in *Journal of Social Development in Africa,* Vol. 19, No.2, 2004, pp. 90-112.

Mba, C.J. 2003a. "Sexual Behaviour and the Risks of HIV/AIDS and other STDs among Young People in Sub-Saharan Africa: A Review" in *Research Review,* vol. 19, No.1, 2003, pp.15-25.

Mba, C.J. 2003b. "The Effect of HIV/AIDS Mortality on Africa's Life Expectancy and Implications for the elderly population: A Case Study of South Africa and Ghana". Paper presented at the International Conference on *Geriatric Care in Africa: Now and the Future,* Cape Town South Africa, 6-8 March 2003.

Mbamaonyeukwu, C.J. 2001a. "The Battle Against AIDS: The Winds are Contrary", in *The Spectator,* Ghana's popular Weekly Newspaper, Saturday March 24, p.3.

Mbamaonyeukwu, C.J. 2001b. "The Ageing of Africa's Populations", in *BOLD* Quarterly Journal of the International Institute on Ageing, vol. 11, No. 4, 2001, pp. 2-7.

Mbamaonyeukwu, C.J. 2000. "AIDS: A Threat to Humanity", in *The Spectator,* Ghana's popular Weekly Newspaper, Saturday Dec. 2, 2000, p.3 & Saturday Dec. 9, p.11.

Miller, N. and Yaeger, R. 1995. "By Virtue of their Occupation, Soldiers and Sailors are at Greater Risk", *AIDS Analysis Africa,* Vol. 9, No. 5, pp. 8-9.

Namboodiri, K. 1991. *Demographic Analysis: A Stochastic Approach.* Academic Press Inc., London.

Namboodiri, K. and Suchindran, C. M. 1987. *Life Table Techniques and Their Applications.* Academic Press Inc., London.

Philipson, T. and Posner, R. 1995. "The Microeconomics of the AIDS Epidemic in Africa", *Population and Development Review* Vol. 21, No 4, pp. 835-848.

Preston, S.H., Heuveline, P. and Guillot, M. 2000. *Demography: Measuring and Modelling Population Processes.* Blackwell Publishers, United Kingdom.

Takyi, B. and Mba, C. 2005. "Implications of the HIV/AIDS Pandemic for Africa's Labour Force", in *The Journal of Management Studies,* (in press).

UNAIDS 2005: *UNAIDS at Country Level: Progress Report.* The WHO, Geneva, Switzerland.

UNAIDS 2002. *Report on the Global HIV/AIDS Epidemic.* The WHO, Geneva, Switzerland.

UNAIDS 2001. *Report on the Global HIV/AIDS Epidemic.* The WHO, Geneva, Switzerland.

UNAIDS/WHO 2005. *AIDS Epidemic Update: December 2004.* Joint United Nations Programme on HIV/AIDS and World Health Organization, Geneva, Switzerland. http://w3.whosea.org/en/Section10

UNAIDS/WHO 2004. *Report on the Global HIV/AIDS Epidemic.* Joint United Nations Programme on HIV/AIDS and World Health Organization, Geneva, Switzerland.

UNAIDS/WHO 2002. *AIDS Epidemic Update: December 2002.* Joint United Nations Programme on HIV/AIDS and World Health Organization, Geneva, Switzerland.

United Nations, 2003. *World Population Prospects, The 2002 Revision Vol. I: Comprehensive Tables.* Department of Economic and Social Affairs, Population Division, ST/ESA/SER.A/222. New York.

United Nations, 2001. *World Population Prospects, The 2000 Revision: Highlights.* Population Division, Department of Economic and Social Affairs, ESA/P/WP.165, New York.

World Health Organization (WHO) 2004. *World Health Report.* http://www3.who.int/whosis/. The WHO, Geneva, Switzerland.

World Health Organization (WHO), 2002. *World Mortality in 2000: Life Tables for 191 Countries.* The WHO, Geneva, Switzerland.

World Health Organization (WHO), 2001. *1997-1999 World Health Statistics Annual.* http://www3.who.int/whosis/. The WHO, Geneva, Switzerland.

Zimbabwe Ministry of Health, 1995. HIV, STD and AIDS Surveillance. *Zimbabwe Quarterly Reports* No. 3.

161

Chapter 7

Women's Empowerment and Health in Ghana

Esther Yaa. Apewokin

Introduction

Women's health is gradually becoming the major global concern it rightly deserves. Every day, at least 1,600 women die worldwide from complications of pregnancy and childbirth. As many as 50 million women experience pregnancy-related complications which at times lead to disability and/or long term illnesses each year and 99% of these women are in developing countries. The age at which women begin and stop child-bearing, the interval between births, the total number of lifetime pregnancies and the socio-cultural and economic circumstances in which women live influence their health status. According to the WHO (2005), maternal mortality is a major indicator that shows the discrepancies between developed and developing countries. Whereas in developed countries about six women die out of every 100,000 live births, in developing countries the rate may be as high as 800,000 per 100,000 live births. It is sad to note that these deaths could have been avoided.

In sub-Sahara Africa there are 13 women living with HIV as against 10 men. Women are infected with HIV at earlier ages than men. Thirty-six young women aged 15-24 years live with HIV against 10 young men. Women's ability to lead a fulfilling life depends on their health. The consequences of poor health of women affect not only the women but the entire household, community and nation, since women are the primary care givers to the sick and children.

This chapter attempts to look at the emergence of empowerment of women at the various UN conferences, as well as the factors that influence the health seeking behaviour of women with particular reference to men, and the necessary policy measures and programmes developed to improve the health of women in Ghana.

Women's Empowerment

Women's empowerment may be defined as the process by which unequal power relations are transformed and women gain greater equality with men. At the Government level, women's empowerment would include the extension of all fundamental social, economic and political rights to women while at the individual level it is the process by which women gain inner power to express and defend their rights, gain greater self-esteem and control over their own lives in personal and social relationships.

Milestone in the establishment of the Rights of Women and Children

The Milestone in the establishment of the Rights of Women and Children began with the 1945 United Nations Charter and the 1948 Universal Declaration of Human Rights which adopted equal rights for both men and women. In the late 1960s, the UN Bodies and International Organizations recognised the right of women to plan the number and spacing of children. The concept of Reproductive Rights was adopted at the 1994 International Conference on Population and Development (ICPD). This was reaffirmed at the 1995 Fourth World Conference on Women, which recognized women's rights as human rights. The 2000 Millennium Declaration has seven of its goals relating to gender issues. Ghana actively participated in these International Conferences and has committed herself to the Conventions that have been adopted. Figure 1 shows the significant milestones dates that have been achieved during the period 1948-2004 in respect of the rights of women and children by the United Nations.

Figure 1. Milestones in the establishment of the rights of women and children

In the 20th century several international treaties came into being, holding signatory countries accountable for the human rights of their citizens. Over the past two decades United Nations bodies as well as international, regional and national courts, have increasingly focused on the human rights of mothers and children.

1984 — The Universal Declaration of Human Rights states "motherhood and childhood are entitled to special care and assistance".

1952 — The General Conference of the International Labour Organization adopts the Maternity Protection Convention

1959 — The Declaration of the rights of the Child.

1966 — The International Covenant on Economics, Social and cultural Rights recognizes the right to the highest attainable standard of physical and mental health.

1981 — The Convention on the Elimination of All Forms of Discrimination Against Women enjoins States parties to ensure appropriate maternal health services.

1989 — The Convention on the Rights of the Child guarantees children right to health. States commit themselves to ensuring appropriate maternal health services

1990 — At the United Nations World Summit on Children governments declare their "joint commitment ..to give every child a better future". And recognize the link between women's rights and children's well-being.

165

1993 — The United Nations Human Rights committee express concern over high rates of maternal mortality.

1994 / 1995 — The United Nations International Conference on Population and Development and the United Nations Fourth World Conference on Women affirm women's right of access to appropriate health care services in pregnancy and childbirth

1996 — The United Nations United Nations Human Right Committee rulers that, when abortion gives rise to a criminal penalty even if a woman is pregnant as a result of rape, a woman's right to be free from inhuman and degrading treatment might be violated.

2000 — The United Nations Committee on Economic, Social and Cultural Rights states that measures are required to "improve child and maternal health, sexual and reproductive health services".

2003 — The United Nations Committee on the Rights of the child states that adolescent girls should have access to information on e impact of early marriage and early pregnancy and have access to health services sensitive to their needs and rights.

2003 — The United Nations Commission on Human Rights, states that sexual and reproductive health are integral elements of the right to health.

e United Nations Committee on the Rights the child adopts its General Comment on V/AIDS and that on the Right of the Child.

2004 — The United Nations Committee Against Torture calls for an end to the extraction of confessions for prosecution purposes from en seeking emergency medical care as a ult of illegal abortion. The United Nations Special Rapporteur on the Right to Health ports that all forms of special violence are inconsistent with the right to health.

2004 — The United Nations Sub-Commission on the Promotion and Protection of Human Rights adopts a resolution on "harmful traditional practices affecting the health of women and the girl child".

Women's Health

Men and women have fundamental rights to health. However, in developing countries good health and well being continue to elude most women throughout their life cycle. They have unequal access to basic health services. The result is an increased risk of unwanted pregnancies, HIV infection and other sexually transmitted infections as well as unsafe abortions and complications related to pregnancy and childbirths. It has been estimated that globally there are 529,000 maternal deaths per year, 48% of which occur in Africa (WHO et al., 2003). Ghana has a maternal mortality ratio (MMR) of 214 per 100,000 live births with pockets of areas where it is as high as 700-800 per 100,000 live births.

The status of women's health is largely reflected in indicators such as maternal mortality and morbidity, disease burden, reproductive health and reproductive behaviour, contraception, abortion, maternal mortality and morbidity, nutrition, work environment and health covering aspects like poor sanitation, air pollution, poor quality of housing, degradation of natural resources, sexual harassment and health problems related to the nature of women's work and violence against women. Malnutrition often poses a serious threat to the life of girls and women. Women's risk of premature death and disability is higher during their reproductive years. High MMRs coupled with low educational levels of women put women in low social and economic status which limits their access to quality health care services including family planning.

The changes through which women go during their reproductive ages affect them throughout their life. Childbearing and nurturing come with its attendant problems. Any delays in seeking prompt medical attention during pregnancy and delivery would affect not only the mother and the child, but also other members of the family.

The 2003 GDHS shows that majority of Ghanaian women irrespective of their marital status do not have

Table 1 Women's participation in decision making

Percent distribution of women by person who has the final say in making specific decisions, according to current marital status and type of decision, Ghana 2003

	Currently married or living together								Not married					
	Woman only	Jointly with husband	Husband only	Husband only	Someone else only	Decision not made/not applicable	Total	Number of women	Woman only	Jointly with someone else	Someone else only	Decision not made/not applicable	Total	Number of women
Own health care	37.0	20.6	0.9	34.9	6.6	0.0	100.0	3,549	33.1	7.3	58.6	1.0	100.0	2,142
Large household purchases	20.9	30.2	1.5	40.9	6.3	0.2	100.0	3,549	25.5	5.9	66.4	2.2	100.0	2,142
Daily household purchases	28.8	32.3	1.4	31.8	5.5	0.2	100.0	3,549	26.5	5.8	65.4	2.3	100.0	2,142
Visits to family or relatives	20.9	37.9	1.5	33.7	5.4	0.5	100.0	3,549	29.6	6.1	62.0	2.3	100.0	2,142
What food to cook each day	39.9	26.5	1.7	26.1	5.6	0.2	100.0	3,549	27.0	7.8	63.1	2.1	100.0	2,142

Note: Percentages may not add to 100 due to the exclusion of women with missing information. Never-married, divorced, separated or widowed women

167

sole authority over the household decision to seek health care for themselves. While a fifth of married women make decisions on their health with their spouses, only a third of married and unmarried women could make sole decisions on their health care without the consent of a male counterpart. Men are generally perceived as household heads and are expected to make major decisions concerning the household with or without their partners.

Other socio-cultural practices such as female genital mutilation, Trokosi, limited spousal communication on reproductive health issues, teenage marriages and pregnancies compromise the health of women. The practice of banishing and condemning women into penal homes on suspicion of witchcraft affects their mental health. Lastly, the betrothal of girls into marriage to elderly men is another concern. The fear of HIV/AIDS in recent time is leading to demand for young bride which compromises on the health of such girls. It has been stated that "The most unfortunate of forced marriages are those involving the betrothal of infants to men of their parents' generation. Among peoples such as the Konkomba who have traditionally practiced these forms of marriage and sister exchanges (whereby two men "swap" sisters as wives), the betrothed husband would have worked for many years to "earn" his future wife. The process may begin even before the birth of the girl when the interested man would have started to woo the foetus in the hope that it turns out to be female. The man in this case provides not only for his future bride's needs but also attends to the demands of her parents and kin. It therefore becomes difficult for a man who has invested so much in a girl to let go when in future upon attaining maturity such a girl decides she would rather have another man for a husband.

It is a scenario that complicates community relations when the girls elope with the men of their choice. Prudence would in the this case dictate that the girl is denied schooling to pre-empt any possibility of her refusing her betrothed husband in future". (United Nations, 2003).

Traditionally women's health services have focused on addressing their reproductive health needs, especially contraception and safe childbearing. The needs of young women and those who are in their menopause are not given the needed attention. Women of child-bearing age have also not found it easy to obtain health care for non-reproductive problems especially mental health care. Women's mental health is poorly addressed. There is increase in psychiatric illnesses in women. Increasingly whereas causative factors of mental health in men is due largely to their lifestyle, in women it is often due to social and marital problems. Gender-based violence particularly domestic violence lead to depression in women. Acts of violence such as rape and battery affect the physical and mental well being of women. The injuries and trauma from these acts may be pervasive and have long-term health complications. Despite these problems women generally live longer than men.

Persistence of cultural beliefs and customs do prevent women from seeking health care. Emotional and cognitive capacities of women themselves may limit their access to health care. Women generally believe that suffering is their lot, therefore problems such as backache or vaginal discharge may be accepted as normal.

Policies and Programmes

In the 1992 Constitution of Ghana is enshrined equal rights for both men and women. The Ghana Poverty Reduction Strategy (GPRS) of 2006 is the blue-print for the socio-economic development of the country. In the current update of the GPRS the effort was made to streamline population, gender and the empowerment of women, as included in the "Vulnerability and Excluded Thematic Area" of the document.

The Government of Ghana has introduced exemption policies for certain categories of the population. Free ante-natal care and delivery have been introduced in the three northern and Central regions. The National Health

Insurance Scheme is also replacing the "Cash and Carry" system. All these efforts are aimed at improving both access and quality of service.

Other policies include the National Population Policy (Revised Edition, 1994). The Draft National Ageing Policy, Adolescent and Reproductive Health Policy, the Gender Policy the HIV/AIDs/STIs Policy, and the Early Childhood Development Policy.

The National Population Council in collaboration with the development partners, Ministry of Health/Ghana Health Service, Ministry of Women and Children's Affairs, International Federation of Women Lawyers, Planned Parenthood Association of Ghana, Women and Juvenile Unit of Ghana Police Service, and Traditional Authorities have developed and implemented pro-grammes to promote an improvement in the health of women with particular reference to reproductive health.

 Challenges

The major constraints to the empowerment of women in accessing health care are socio-cultural, poverty, and low educational status of women. To empower women there is the need to educate girls to the secondary school level and beyond. Education empowers girls to be assertive delay marriage improve nutritional values of their families and motivate them to have small family sizes. Indeed, education is a key factor in reproductive health decisions.

Lastly women cannot be empowered if they continue to live in poverty. Poverty leads to sexual exploitation. Indeed, for millions of women across the world sex is the price which they are expected to pay for many of life's opportunities, from gaining admission to overcrowded classrooms to passing examinations and securing employment.

In conclusion according to Dr. John Grant, a former Executive Director of UNICEF, "there is something very wrong, something obscene and hypocritical about a world that universally exalts motherhood and yet permits hundreds of thousands of maternal deaths year in and year out from causes that are now largely preventable. There is something very wrong about a world that tells women that motherhood is their route to realisation and status and yet denies so many of them the means to prevent or remedy the dangerous complications that can be associated with pregnancy and child birth".

Empowerment of women does not lower the status of men but rather enhances it. Let us together push the Cairo and Beijing Agenda forward.

References

Ghana AIDS Commission, 2004. *National HIV/AIDS and STI Policy.* Accra.

Ghana Health Service, 2003. *National Reproductive Health Service, Policy and Standards, Second Edition.* Accra.

Ghana Statistical Service, Macro International Inc., 1999. *Ghana Demographic and Health Survey, 1998, Calverton, Maryland USA.*

Government of Ghana, Ministry of Women and Children's Affairs, 2005, *National Gender and Children Policy.*

Government of Ghana, UNICEF, 2000, *Situation Analysis of Children and Women in Ghana 2000.*

Government of Ghana, Ministry of Youth and Sports 1999. *National Youth Policy.* Accra.

Government of Ghana, Ghana Health Service 2003. *National Reproductive Health Service Policy and Standards* (revised edition). Accra.

Government of Ghana, Ghana Statistical Service. *Ghana Child Labour Survey Report, 2003.*

Government of Ghana. 1992 Constitution.

National AIDS/STI Control Programme, Ghana Health Service, Ghana AIDS Commission, 2004. *HIV/AIDS in Ghana: Current Situation Projections Impacts, Interventions.*

National Population Council, 1994, *National Population Policy (Revised Edition).* Accra.

National Population Council, 2000, *Adolescent Reproductive Health Policy.* Accra.

UNFPA/Government of Ghana, 2004. *State of Ghana Population Report 2003, Population Poverty and Development.*

UNFPA/Government of Ghana, 2004. *UNFPA/Government of Ghana Fourth Country Programme 2001-2005: Mid-Term Review Country Brief. (Unpublished).*

United Nations, 1995. *Report of the International Conference on Population and Development.* Cairo 5-13 September 1994, New York.

Chapter 8

Population and Health Care Facilities in Ghana

Frank Nyonator

Introduction

The Health Status of Ghanaians has been improving since independence, however, the rate of change has been slowing and current health service indicators are still far from desirable. Maternal mortality rates, child mortality and morbidity rates remains high; malaria and other communicable diseases including HIV/AIDS are persistent. Between 1957 and 1988 Ghana's child and infant mortality rates declined from 154 to 110 and 133 to 57 per 1,000 live births, respectively. These declines however have stopped or been reversed in the past few years. In 2003, child mortality rates were 111 per 1000 live births, approximately the same as in 1988; while Infant Mortality increased to 64 over the same time period. So, despite substantial investments in expanding and upgrading the network of government health facilities, evidence for increased uptake of health services is mixed.

Extending the coverage of basic and primary health care services to all Ghanaians has been the major objective of the Ministry of Health since the Alma Ata Conference on "Health for All" in 1977. A major policy statement of the Ministry of Health in 1977 was that "most disease problems that cause the high rates of illness and deaths among Ghanaians are preventable or curable if diagnosed promptly by simple basic and primary health care procedures. The major objectives (of the Ministry) are to extend coverage of basic and primary health services to as many people as possible during the next ten years. In order to provide this extent of coverage it will be necessary to engage the co-operation and authorization of the people themselves at the community level. It will involve virtual curtailment of the sophisticated hospital construction and renovation and will require a re-orientation and re-deployment of at least some of the health personnel from hospital-based activities to community-oriented activities." (National Health Planning Unit, 1977).

The strategic policy direction of the Ghana Health Service is to have a three tier level of service provision within a district – the District (Hospital) Level, the Sub-District (Health Centre) Level and Community-based. As captured in the Medium Term Health Strategy, geographical access is a major barrier to health care and as such, the first and second five-year programmes of works had set out to improve geographic access to services by building new facilities to expand the government owned facility network.

In line with this health service delivery strategy, the number of facilities doubled over the first and second five-year programmes of work at the sub-district and district levels, but exacerbated by the 'brain drain', the investment in 'sub-district structures' did not remove the barriers to health care. From independence to the early 1980s there was a rapid expansion of government-owned facilities with the assumption that these will benefit the poor by increasing geographic access to relatively low priced services. However, uptake of services has not improved. Indeed an analysis of all key service delivery indicators shows a disturbing trend in the current uptake of health facilities by the population. The average Bed Occupancy (BO) rates from most of the Ghana Health Service (GHS) facilities are about 53%. Outpatient attendance is stagnating and supervised delivery is low.

Trends in Outpatient Department (OPD) attendance per capita for the period 1995-2004 are shown in Figure 1. In general, there has been a consistent increase in OPD attendance per capita from 32% in 1995 to 52% in 2004. Also, antenatal coverage fell from 97% in 2000 to

89% in 2004, supervised delivery fluctuated between 49% and 53%, while family planning coverage rose from 12% to 24% over the same period (Figure 2).

Figure 1: Trend in OPD Attendance Per Capita (Ghana, 1995 – 2004

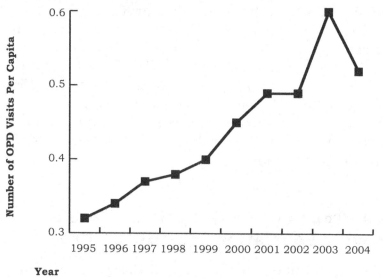

Figure 2: Trend in Antenatal, Supervised Family Planning Coverage 2000 – 2004

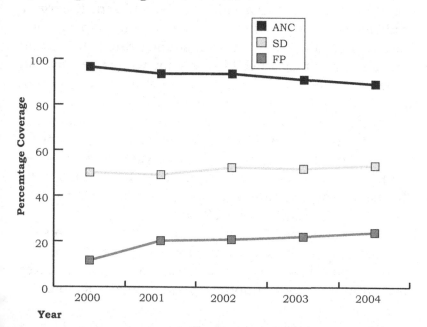

Population and Health Care Facilities in Ghana

Improving the health status of the poor is crucial for poverty reduction in any country, given that ill health is a consequence and cause of poverty. However, in most developing countries like Ghana geographical access is a major barrier to health care. In Ghana a significant proportion of the people still do not have access to health services and where the services are available, the cost of these services deters them from using them. Access in this context, is defined as living within one hour travel time (by any available means) from the health facility. By this definition the government estimates that only 45% of the rural population have access to health services. Nationally, about 40% of the population do not have access to health facilities (Ghana National Development Planning Commission, 2005).

What Type of Health Systems Does a Growing Population Like Ghana Need?

The trends noted above, with all things being equal, indicate that most of our facilities are under utilised. This has led to public health experts questioning the rationale in the continuing investment in huge health facilities, which are invariably under-utilised. Emerging evidence points to the fact that the majority of people living in communities do not want sophisticated clinics and hospitals. What they need is someone who is nearby and knowledgeable to tell them what is wrong, what action to take, and where to go to become healthy.

The ancient and powerful mechanisms of community organization, chieftaincy lineage, social networks, women societies, communication systems and other institutions and stakeholders need to be mobilised by the health system for developing primary health care operations (Nyonator et al, 2005a).

It is obvious that the growing population needs a shift in paradigm in the way that services are provided. The shift in paradigm needs to focus on achieving three important objectives: improving equity in access to basic health services; improving efficiency and responsiveness to client needs; and developing effective inter-sectoral collaboration.

Indeed, the shift in paradigm is guided by the fact that the primary producers of health are the individual households with mothers often taking the first key decision to seek health care for their sick children. This decision to seek health care, and which health care is sought, depends on information available to the household. Communities provide the social cohesion in which families function. And to increase the uptake of health services by households, it is necessary to provide health information and education to the households in a way that is acceptable and convenient for them.

Therefore, in attempting to address the fundamental challenges in both access and quality of care and household/community or demand side participation in service provision, health system policy reform in Ghana should focus on the mobilisation of health care resources and the traditional society to achieve the end points of increased health status, decreased mortality and fertility. This is to be done in the context of the strategic pillars of health sector reform - improving access and gender equity, enhancing quality, developing efficiency, fostering partnership and sustaining financing of service delivery.

Overall, many people believe that it is now important to develop the community-based level to focus on the client and community orientation of the services and to tailor services to individual and community needs and wishes – the 'close-to-client' service delivery system.

In an effort to provide the community–based level, or 'close-to-client' doorstep health delivery with household and community involvement, the Ministry of Health through the Ghana Health Service pioneered the implementation of a national programme to replicate the results of Navrongo Community Health and Family Planning Project (CHFP) known as the Community-based Health Planning and Services (CHPS) initiative in key pilot districts of Nkwanta, Birim North and Asebu-

Abura-Kwamankese (Nyonator et al. 2005b).

Within the context of the Ghana Poverty Reduction Strategy (GPRS), community-based health service delivery using the CHPS approach provides a unique opportunity for achieving the critical intermediate performance measures of the health sector programme areas of work.

The CHPS initiative is therefore the national strategy for implementing community based service delivery by reorienting and relocating primary health care from sub-district health centres to convenient community locations. The CHPS organisational change process relies upon community resources for construction labour, service delivery, and programme oversight. As such, it is a national mobilisation of grass-roots action and leadership in health service delivery. The community-based level service provision will enable the Ghana Health Service (GHS) to reduce health inequalities and promote equity of health outcomes by removing geographic barriers to health care. The CHPS is a component of other government policy agendas, such as the GPRS which identifies CHPS as a key element in pro-poor health services, as well as the ruling Party's Manifesto which identifies CHPS as a priority health activity. In addition, various health sector performance reviews since 2002 commended CHPS as an appropriate way to deliver health care to communities in undeveloped and deprived areas distant from health facilities.

Implementation of and Infrastructure to Deliver the CHPS Intervention

In implementing CHPS, it is proposed that each sub-district would be divided into at least six zones. Given that each sub-district is carved to contain around a population of 30,000 people, and each zone will have a population of between 500 and 5,000 people or three to four unit committees grouped together. Accordingly, each district will theoretically be divided into at least 48 zones.

This proposal envisages at least 5,280 CHPS zones, which require about 5,280 community health officer's (CHO) to man the system nationally.

In line with the expected roll out of CHPS strategy, about 4475 community health compounds need to be constructed at the community level (Table 1). Working on the assumption that each sub-district will be adequately served by a well equipped and appropriately staffed, and also on the assumption that each district has an average of six sub-Districts, a total of 346 additional health centres will need to be constructed at the sub-district level. A properly located District Hospital will be expected to provide adequate referral support for the sub-district health structures and taking into consideration the existing 72 district hospitals (Public and Mission Institutions), an additional 67 district hospitals are needed to be constructed at the district level. With the kind of health systems outlined, each region will need a referral hospital. The current situation will require the refurbishment of some of existing regional hospitals and the construction of a 'Regional Hospital', for instance, for the Ashanti Region.

Table 1: Estimated number of facilities to support a 'whole District Health Systems

Level	Number of Facilities needed	Current Situation	Additional Structures Needed
Community level – Community compounds	6 CHC's X 6 Sub Districts X 139 Districts = 4896	47 + (374 Clinics)	4,475
Sub-district Level - Health Centres	6 Health Centres X 139 Districts = 834	488	346
District Hospitals	139 District Hospitals	62 + 10	67
Regional Hospitals	10	9	1
Teaching Hospitals		2	

Conclusion

To meet the health needs of the growing population of Ghana, and in the face of limited resources, it is recommended that Government uses available funds to build facilities that can make an impact. It therefore presupposes that a high level of prioritisation towards building the community level facilities, and the political will to strike a balance in the construction of facilities within a health system that will make the maximum impact and to resist the temptation of constructing 'visible' edifices that do not meet the needs of the population and which may be underutilised.

Clearly, tertiary health structures such as regional hospitals and tertiary institutions are needed to provide the backup support within a comprehensive health system. However, a balance in investment is needed so as to channel the bulk of funds to build more health centres and create functional CHPS zones. This will go a long way to serve the growing population better.

A comparison of the 'estimated number of facilities' needed to support the development of the 'whole district health systems' (about 4,889) and the existing facilities (Annex 1) of about 2740 is revealing.

It is recommended that the numbers of health facilities available need to be doubled. Furthermore, the bulk of these facilities should be sited at the community and sub-district levels in order to make any impact on the health of the growing population of Ghana and achieve the country's Millennium Development Goals.

References

Ghana Health Service, 2005. *Facts and Figures for 2004*. PPMED 2005.

Ghana National Development Planning Commission, 2005. *The Ghana Macro-economics and Health Initiative (GMHI)*. In Print.

National Health Planning Unit (NHPU), 1977. *Health Policies for Ghana*. NHPU, Ghana Health Service, Accra.

Nyonator, Frank K, Tanya C. Jones, Robert A. Miller, James F. Phillips, J Koku Awoonor-Williams. 2005 (a). "Guiding the Ghana Community-based Health Planning and Services Approach to Scaling up with Qualitative Systems Appraisal. *International Quarterly of Community Health Education* (CHE). Vol. 23, No.3, 2004-2005.

Nyonator, Frank K, J Koku Awoonor-Williams, James F. Phillips, Tanya C. Jones, Robert A. Miller. 2005 (b). "The Ghana Community-based Health Planning and Services Initiative for Scaling up Service Delivery Innovation. *Health Policy and Planning* 20 (1): 25-34.

Nyonator, Frank; Dovlo Dela, Ken Sagoe, 2004. "The Health of the Nation and the Brain Drain in the Health Sector". Paper presented at the UNDP sponsored Conference on Migration and Development in Ghana. September 14-16, 2004. Accra.

Annex 1. Current State of Health Infrastructure in Ghana: Health Facilities by Type and Ownership, 2004

Region	Teaching Hospital	Regional Hospital	District Hospitals		Other Hospitals				Poly clinic	Health Centres				Clinics and Maternity Homes				Regional Total
			Govt	Mission	Govt	Mission	Quasi Govt	Private	Govt	Govt	Mission	Quasi Govt	Private	Govt	Mission	Quasi Govt	Private	
Western	0	1	9	2	1	3	6	0	2	54	0	0	0	69	29	27	108	311
Central	0	1	8	3	1	1	1	7	0	44	0	0	0	56	23	1	118	264
Greater Accra	1	1	2	0	6	1	9	58	7	35	2	1	0	20	2	6	159	310
Volta	0	1	10	1	1	7	1	5	1	199	6	0	0	65	11	0	31	339
Eastern	0	1	9	2	3	3	3	6	0	58	14	1	0	158	7	6	119	390
Ashanti	1	0	15	3	7	11	4	41	0	96	2	0	0	53	47	2	164	446
Brong Ahafo	0	1	5	6	0	4	1	8	0	36	0	0	0	96	9	7	78	251
Northern	0	1	5	3	2	1	2	1	0	95	17	1	1	31	19	4	11	194
Upper East	0	1	4	1	0	0	0	0	0	25	5	0	0	74	12	1	10	133
Upper West	0	1	3	1	0	3	0	1	0	50	12	0	5	18	4	0	4	102
Total	2	9	70	22	21	35	27	127	10	692	57	3	6	640	163	54	805	2,740

Source: CHIM/PPME-GHS

NB Maternity homes are classified as clinic.

182

Chapter 9

Conclusion

Stephen O. Kwankye and Chuks J. Mba

The papers that were presented at the Seminar raised a number of relevant developmental issues and generated a wide range of discussions. A number of recommendations and conclusions were also made. The salient features of these discussions and concomitant recommendations are presented in this chapter.

First, it is important to undertake more qualitative studies to investigate the factors that are responsible for the fertility transition in Ghana, considering that the socio-cultural environment plays critical roles in shaping fertility behaviour, choices and decisions not only in Ghana but throughout sub-Saharan Africa. For now however, efforts should be made to develop the large army of youthful population into a useful human resource for nation building.

In all the presentations, education has been highlighted as a key factor towards the achievement of almost all the MDGs. In response to this recognition therefore, while ensuring that all children of school going age go to school, equally adequate attention should be paid to adult literacy. This is important considering the high rate of early school drop out especially among females in the rural areas. Formal education alone may not provide us with the full antidote.

The analysis of HIV prevalence across sub-Saharan Africa suggests quite plausibly that poor countries are not necessarily those with the highest rates of HIV infection. It is therefore not quite clear the extent to which poverty stands to blame as a major cause of HIV. While this may appear to be a valid argument at the country by country comparison, within each country, the situation may be to the contrary and poverty may be a very important factor or condition in understanding HIV infection and spread although the role of other conditions and factors like education cannot be discounted. The need for more research in this area cannot also be underestimated.

There appears to be a conflict between the policy environment and the legal framework regarding sexuality and contraception. While the policy makes it clear that all sexually active adolescents (i.e., 10-19-year-olds) should have access to contraception, the law on defilement rules out sexual consent by persons less than 16 years. By implication, persons less than 16 years cannot and should not be sexually active and are therefore not eligible to have access to, or use any form of contraception in Ghana. This is a clear conflict, which requires resolution to guide institutions and organisations like the Ghana Social Marketing Foundation (GSMF), which are into contraceptive advocacy, provision and sensitisation programmes.

Again, there are still concerns about condom educational campaigns as a way of counteracting the upsurge of HIV/AIDS in Ghana and elsewhere in Africa. With reference to young persons however, this practice is clearly in conflict with Ghana's law on defilement. Consequently, there should be audience segmentation, which should seek to place emphasis on abstinence for young persons to keep them away from early sex and condoms for persons who are sexually active beyond the age at which one could have consent for sex as is enshrined in the laws of the state.

From the papers and discussions at the Seminar, one issue on which consensus was again reached is preventive as opposed to curative health. While efforts at encouraging the population to adopt the use of insecticide treated bed nets are ongoing and ought to be intensified, we need to equally intensify public education and attitudinal change regarding environmental sanitation and the sustainability of the eco-system as a critical component of sustainable development. Garbage collection in our cities and towns should be regular while choked drains ought to be de-silted frequently. As a permanent solution, newly constructed drains should be covered and persons who indiscriminately litter the environment should be prosecuted and heavy fines imposed without delay to serve as deterrent to others.

All indicators of the health status of the population appear to be poor in the three northern regions in Ghana, i.e., Northern, Upper East and Upper West. Yet, there are several interventions that are ongoing in these regions by government and several non-governmental organisations (NGOs). In these regions, we have high fertility because among other things, infant mortality is high. The situation in these regions should however, not be misconstrued to indicate a failure of the interventions. This is because demographic phenomena often require long periods of time to register tangible changes.

In the area of women empowerment, the focus should not be on economic power only but power over their sexual behaviour and decisions as well. This is against the backdrop of the fact that sexual and reproductive health should be seen as human rights.

It is furthermore important to note that while malnutrition especially in children should be an issue of grave concern to us as a nation, we should equally be concerned about the increasing dependence of a sizable proportion of the population (especially in the urban areas) on fast foods, which have the potential to increase the cholesterol and obesity levels of consumers who live almost sedentary lifestyles with little or no physical exercise. There is therefore the urgent need to intensify educational campaigns to encourage regular consumers of fast foods to either make physical exercise a regular activity or cut down on their intake of fast foods. At the same time, standards should be set for fast foods operators regarding the fat and oil content of their food supplies.

The issue of late antenatal attendance at health facilities during pregnancy came up in one of the papers presented. The concern during discussions was whether it was the result of the absence of user-friendly service delivery or the inadequate knowledge about the relevance of early antenatal care among the population. While encouraging pregnant women to regularly attend antenatal clinic, efforts should be made to ensure that services at various health facilities are user-friendly to encourage high attendance. Besides, people should be educated on the Health Charter that highlights the rights of clients so that the clients would be able to insist on their rights for better services and friendly reception at the facilities. It should also be possible for people who feel unfairly treated to seek redress from constitutionally established institutions including the Commission for Human Rights and Administrative Justice (CHRAJ).

It is however, important to have a study that attempts to show the relationship between the number of antenatal visits and pregnancy outcomes. Such a study could be a critical tool for antenatal care advocacy and behaviour change communication.

"Wife battering" is often explained in the context of traditional norms and practices that tend to suggest that the wife should always be seen to be submissive irrespective of the physical and psychological harm she may be subjected to in the home. Such a situation is frustrating efforts at ensuring that perpetrators of women battering are punished wherever the act occurs. Traditional societal norms and practices should therefore not become immovable impediments in the passage of the domestic violence bill into law.

Furthermore, a clear link was established between increasing population and water inadequacy. What should be noted is that the inadequacy is not just an issue of technology and money but most importantly slowing down of population growth and attitudinal change in the handling of water from the perspective of both producers and consumers. This explains why in spite of all efforts made in the water sector especially towards guinea worm eradication Ghana still ranks high as one of the guinea worm endemic countries in sub-Saharan Africa.

With regard to brain drain of medical professionals, the suggestion was that basic medical training should be tailored to the disease profile of the society especially within the rural setting. There should in addition be a few medical specialists. Such a system would allow for the training of more and more health personnel to handle all the infections and diseases that are common in the context of the environment we find ourselves and at the same time, provide avenues for the medical personnel to rely on the few specialists for advice and direction any time they are confronted with new health problems that may emerge. There is therefore no need for too many medical specialists as we could rely on telemedicine if it is properly planned and developed with doctors in the rural areas having easy link with the specialists whenever it becomes necessary. What we need to decide as a nation is the kind of health system we want and invest in it.

Perhaps, the time has come for Ghana to emulate the unique example of the Cuban doctors who are trained to handle "Cuban diseases" and to work in teams to solve complex problems they may not be familiar with. The need then arises for the Ministry of Health to study the Cuban system of training of medical officers to see to what extent it would be applicable to the Ghanaian situation.

Another area of health care or service delivery is the role of traditional medicine as opposed to modern scientific medicine. This is because increasingly, whether as a result of poverty or perceived efficacy of traditional herbal preparations, more and more people are resorting to traditional herbal medication as an alternative to modern medicine. Whether the state recognises it or not, traditional medicine is fast gaining grounds in our health care delivery system. It is thus important that it is recognised and ways fashioned to ensure that it is hygienically produced and is safe for not only human consumption but certified to be able to treat the diseases or infections for which it is intended. The preparations should however be examined and passed under laboratory tests to be effective before being allowed on the open market.

Finally, there appear to be no regular fora for sharing scientific ideas and results or findings from the numerous research works that have been done over the years. Whenever these fora have been created, they are usually among the research community members to talk to themselves and not with the population that is studied. As much as possible therefore, platforms should be created at the community level to share research findings as part of the sensitisation and educational campaigns as well as share best practices.

In sum, the issues raised bring to the fore the challenges that face us as developing countries towards the attainment of the MDGs. Thankfully, these challenges are surmountable if the state is committed to addressing them with the population also ready to lend its support to the programmes while at the same time responding to behaviour and attitudinal change in every sphere of life.

Endnotes

1   Replacement-level fertility rate is defined as a total fertility of 2.1 children per woman, which includes one-tenth of a child extra to make up for the mortality of children and of women who do not reach the end of the reproductive years.

2   The decline in the overall dependency ratio that occurs during the early phase of fertility decline has been described as "demographic bonus" because, during this period, the money that would otherwise be spent supporting dependents can be saved and invested to promote economic development.

3   Effect of abortion is assumed to be zero.

4   Information gathered from water engineers at Water Research Institute and Ghana Water Company.

5   Ibid.

6   Figure is based on both rural and small towns.

7   level 1:no access (quantity of water collected often less than 5 litres per capita per day[l/c/d]) and level 2{ basic access (average quantity unlikely to exceed 20 l/c/d)

8   Intermittency of water supply forces residents who are supposed to have access to pipe borne to resort to unprotected sources [rivers, lakes etc.]

9   The severely affected African countries are Angola, Benin, Botswana, Burkina Faso, Burundi, Cameroon, Central African Republic, Chad, Congo (Democratic Republic), Congo (Republic), Djibouti, Eritrea, Ethiopia, Gabon, Gambia, Ghana, Guinea-Bissau, Ivory Coast, Kenya, Lesotho, Liberia, Malawi, Mali, Mozambique, Namibia, Nigeria, Rwanda, Sierra Leone, South Africa, Swaziland, Tanzania, Togo, Uganda, Zambia, and Zimbabwe (United Nations, 2001).

10 Also, because Ghana's population rose from 12,296,081 in 1984 to 18,912,079 in 2000, a population growth rate of 2.7% per annum by the exponential method would have been assumed (the use of the exponential approach is predicated on the fact that it more accurately describes the nature of population growth as a continuous process, going on all the time; see for example, Mba, 2002; Mbamaonyeukwu, 1990).

11 In the absence of reliable empirical evidence, this assumption seems plausible since both Ghana and South Africa share similar traditional and other characteristics.

12 The proportion is arrived at by simply applying the Waring-Lagrange extrapolation technique to the information supplied (Shyrock and Siegel, 1976).

13 That is, (5595/72564)*100=7.7%; (5580/48471)*100=11.5%.

14 It is important to remember that the HIV/AIDS prevalence rates are not taken into account in the determination of mortality profile as shown in Tables 1a and 1b.